"More workplaces should be experimenting with the four-day work-week. *Do More in Four* reveals why and how."

—ADAM GRANT, #1 *New York Times* bestselling author, *Think Again* and *Hidden Potential*; podcast host, *Re:Thinking*

"Some books nudge you. *Do More in Four* challenges everything you assume about effort, efficiency, and the modern workweek. It's both a sharp critique of outdated norms and a hopeful blueprint for what's next."

—DANIEL H. PINK, #1 *New York Times* bestselling author, *When* and *Drive*

"*Do More in Four* offers an important and compelling case for reimagining the modern workweek. With clarity and insight, this utterly engaging book challenges conventional wisdom and offers a practical road map to greater productivity and well-being. A must-read for leaders serious about building smarter, healthier organizations."

—AMY C. EDMONDSON, professor, Harvard Business School; author, *Right Kind of Wrong* and *The Fearless Organization*

"Ready to rethink the way we work? A bold, inspiring call to action for a more sustainable workweek and backed by research and real-world examples, *Do More in Four* shows why the four-day workweek isn't just possible—it's inevitable. Whether you're a business leader, policy maker, or curious professional, it offers a compelling vision for how fewer working hours can truly be more."

—JOSH BERSIN, founder and CEO, The Josh Bersin Company

"The fight for a four-day workweek is one of the most civilizing and important battles of our time, and this excellent book will add rocket fuel to it."

—JOHANN HARI, *New York Times* bestselling author, *Lost Connections* and *Stolen Focus*

"While a four-day workweek may not work for every company, Joe O'Connor and Jared Lindzon offer a compelling vision and practical strategies that challenge leaders to reimagine how work gets done. They make a strong case for designing organizations that deliver results while giving people more time for life. In the future, we should be able to create more value by working less."

—ANNIE DEAN, Vice President, Workplace + Future of Work Transformation, Atlassian

"*Do More in Four* is one of those awakening and incisive reads that makes you want to pamphleteer its message around every workplace. It's like rolling suitcases in an age of handheld luggage: there's so clearly a better way, if only we open our eyes to it."

—BREE GROFF, author, *Today Was Fun: A Book About Work (Seriously)*

"Joe O'Connor and Jared Lindzon's *Do More in Four* shows that less can be more. Measuring success by goals, not hours, is key to preventing burnout, boosting retention, and giving people the space to do meaningful work. Any leader who wants to remain relevant in the future of work should read this book."

—JENNIFER MOSS, workplace culture strategist; award-winning author, *Unlocking Happiness at Work, The Burnout Epidemic,* and *Why Are We Here?*

"*Do More in Four* is a book you should read before your competitors do. It proves the four-day workweek is more strategy than perk. O'Connor and Lindzon back it up with global research, real companies, and breathtaking results. A vital read if you care about your employees."

—DAN PONTEFRACT, award-winning author, *Work-Life Bloom, Flat Army,* and *Lead. Care. Win.*

"Joe O'Connor and Jared Lindzon offer a tantalizing solution to the burnout epidemic of the so-called infinite workday: shorter hours at the same rate of pay, with better performance. Wishful thinking? On the contrary, *Do More in Four* is chock-full of sharp arguments, unassailable data, compelling case studies, and engaging stories. It provides battle-tested strategies for how a shorter workweek can work and why it's more important than ever."

—BRIGID SCHULTE, Pulitzer Prize–winning journalist; *New York Times* bestselling author, *Overwhelmed: Work, Love, and Play When No One Has the Time*; and Director, Better Life Lab, New America

"The most effective teams in the world have discovered a counterintuitive secret: a shorter workweek produces better results. *Do More in Four* exposes why our obsession with long hours is killing both performance and profits. It provides a proven road map for organizations ready to outpace their competition while giving employees their lives back."

—JEN FISHER, founder and CEO, The Wellbeing Team; coauthor, bestselling *Work Better Together*

"Achieving more in less time is the holy grail of management advice. Two world-leading experts on work-time reduction show you how you can indeed 'do more in four,' with a brilliant guide to preparing for, implementing, assessing, and sustaining this revolutionary schedule. A must-read for anyone in the world of work."

—JULIET SCHOR, *New York Times* bestselling author, *The Overworked American*

"For most people, work overpowers life. The balance they crave remains elusive for their entire careers because the scope creep of work feels impossible to defeat. In this wonderful book, Joe O'Connor and Jared Lindzon prove that reclaiming your personal life as a priority is possible—and I can't think of a more important message. The number two regret of dying people is: 'I wish I hadn't worked so hard,' because work was never meant to dominate the mosaic of a meaningful life. Give the people you care about this important manual now!"

—JULIET FUNT, founder and CEO, Juliet Funt Group; author, *A Minute to Think*

"This book is a wake-up call for leaders who want to evolve from outdated norms to our current and future realities. *Do More in Four* proves that a thriving culture and breakthrough performance don't require more time—just better thinking."

    —CY WAKEMAN, *New York Times* bestselling author,
    Reality-Based Leadership

"The businesses that want to lead the future are adopting more flexible ways to work. *Do More in Four* is a road map for leaders who aren't chained to the way things have always been done. It should be essential reading for CEOs."

    —KATHLEEN DAVIS, former Deputy Editor, *Fast Company*; podcast host,
    The New Way We Work

DO MORE
IN FOUR

To:

Subject:

From: Automatic reply: OUT OF OFFICE

DO MORE IN FOUR

Why It's Time for a Shorter Workweek

Joe O'Connor
Jared Lindzon

Harvard Business Review Press
Boston, Massachusetts

Copyright 2026 Joe O'Connor and Jared Lindzon

Printed in the United States of America

10 9 8 7 6 5 4 3 2 1

The web addresses referenced in this book were live and correct at the time of the book's publication but may be subject to change.

Cataloging-in-Publication data is forthcoming.

ISBN: 979-8-89-279-145-8
eISBN: 979-8-89279-146-5

The paper used in this publication meets the requirements of the American National Standard for Permanence of Paper for Publications and Documents in Libraries and Archives Z39.48-1992.

In loving memory of Joe's late parents, Bob and Margaret O'Connor.
And to Jared's daughter Beatrice Lindzon, who was born during the writing of this book.

Contents

Part Three

The Four-Day Blueprint
How to Do More in Four

PART ONE

———————

The Case for Four

Why It's Time for a Shorter Workweek

.

1 Why the Future Is Four

The expression "May you live in interesting times" is meant as both a blessing and a curse.

The phrase, which is believed to have Chinese origins, speaks to the belief that there are often long stretches of history where little happens, followed by short bursts of rapid change. It acknowledges that those periods of turmoil can be difficult but often give way to a better future. Like it or not, we live in interesting times.

The exact starting point is open to debate, but historians are likely to look back on this era as the latest period of upheaval and change, of rapid technological innovation and disruption, of changing preferences and perspectives, and of a growing demand to reevaluate our relationship with work.

Over two hundred years ago, another "interesting" period changed labor from the very human activities our species had engaged in previously—starting from roughly the beginning of human existence—to something that was much more rigid. It took people out of nature and into cities, out of their family units and into an anonymous mass of workers, out of a reliance on the things that made us human and into a reliance on things that made us more like machines. We have long moved on from that economy, yet many of its workplace norms, standards, and practices remain.

Now, during these interesting times, we have an opportunity to get back some of what was lost. This book will seek to demonstrate that transitioning the standard five-day workweek to four—without adjusting employee compensation or employer expectations—is one of the most effective ways for individuals, businesses, and societies to address some of the problems that stem from that last major period of upheaval.

We might not feel all that lucky to have experienced years of social isolation during the pandemic, and to be living through a time of political unrest, climate change, and severe economic inequality. But the disaster will be even greater if we fail to utilize the uniqueness of this moment to challenge the status quo. The pandemic was devastating, and much of what we lost during that period will never be returned. But if some of those days lost to restrictions ultimately serve to give us—and all future generations—more days free to live our lives to the fullest, we may ultimately look back at that difficult period as not just tragic, but a transformative step toward positive, lasting change.

Whether technology will make us more efficient and productive is hardly worth debating; it has consistently increased human output for the last century, and artificial intelligence (AI) is already enabling early adopters to do so much more.

This incredibly powerful new technology, however, is still in its infancy—we've only experienced the slow, clunky, not-so-user-friendly iPhone 3G version of AI. Just imagine what the iPhone 17 Pro Max version will look like. There is no question that it will supercharge our ability to get things done, and those effects are already starting to be felt. The only question that remains is, who in our society will benefit from those gains? If recent history is any guide, it won't be those at the bottom who continue to work longer hours with less economic stability despite skyrocketing productivity. We believe that sharing those gains will improve not just the lives of individual workers and society as a whole but the fate of organizations as well.

According to a large and growing body of research, the most productive workers, organizations, and economies aren't those that work the longest hours but those that make the most out of the hours they work. If you measure productivity in hours, the four-day workweek represents a significant loss. If you measure productivity in business impact, it could represent a massive gain. As we continue to evolve toward an increasingly knowledge-based economy, organizations will more heavily rely on their employees' most human traits, and those abilities can only be maximized in an environment that balances work with ample rest and recovery.

Through countless trials and studies, surveys and testimonies, research projects and real-world experiences, the data is clear. The organizations that will ultimately thrive in the age of AI will be those that develop healthy workplace cultures, attract and retain the best and brightest talent, maintain a strong gender balance in their leadership ranks, tackle the root causes of burnout, empower employees to do their best work free from distraction, and offer sufficient time off from work in order to recharge or dream up more creative solutions to unique challenges. In the age of AI, the age of work-life balance, the age of talent scarcity, the age of new and unexpected challenges, the top-performing organizations will utilize the four-day workweek to empower their teams, make the most out of every working hour, and ultimately do more in four days than their competitors accomplish in five.

In interesting times, maintaining the status quo in the face of rapidly changing conditions is more radical than adaptation. The view that we should continue working the hours that were set as standard in 1940 during the age of AI is radical. The fact that our dominant work structures are the same today as they were a century ago—when labor outputs were mostly physical, when humans were valued for their most robotic traits, and when women made up less than 20 percent of the workforce—is radical.

In the pages ahead, we'll consider the origins of the five-day workweek and question whether the standard set over a century ago still suits modern realities. We will explore the origins of the four-day workweek movement and break down the research and data that has been generated by academics, analysts, and pioneering organizations since. We will consider the four-day workweek within the context of the AI revolution and the changing generational attitudes toward work. We'll question whether we're measuring productivity in a way that suits modern business realities and explore how the four-day workweek offers a solution to some of society's greatest challenges—including gender equality, declining birth rates, and climate change.

Then we'll meet some of the early adopters of the four-day workweek—organizations that represent a wide range of business sizes, industries, and geographical locations and that engaged in the experiment, seeking and measuring a broad array of business outcomes. Next, we'll provide some research-backed advice and battle-tested best practices for advocating for a four-day workweek, implementing it at an organizational level, and adopting some of its most important principles in your own work. Finally, we'll make one last case for why we believe four days is the future of work.

Organizations can't simply remove a full day of work from their staff's weekly schedule and expect the same results. However, with the right approach, the four-day workweek offers a tool for addressing some of their greatest challenges faster and more effectively than otherwise possible. When implemented properly, less work time can indeed yield greater business results. This book will outline that approach and demonstrate how it can offer significantly better outcomes for businesses, their employees, and society at large.

2 How We Arrived at Five

There is no good reason for the workweek to be five days long.

In fact, there really is no good reason for our weeks to be 7 days long, either. Beyond the Judeo-Christian creation story, there is no celestial rationale for dividing the week into 7 days—as there is for organizing the months. Nor are there any natural patterns that prescribe to a 7-day cycle—as there is for our 365.25-day years. Once humanity chose to organize society around a 7-day week, however, it became very difficult to imagine anything different, and the same is true of our 5-day workweek.

Unlike the 7-day week, the 5-day workweek doesn't even claim its roots in any historic texts or religious practices. Nobody sat down to conduct an objective analysis of the optimal number of days for humanity to work and rest and determined that the current 5-2 split was right or fair or necessary. In fact, the 5-day workweek's history is surprisingly recent and arbitrary, and it has no natural, religious, or celestial purpose for remaining. Like the value of a dollar or Peter Pan's fairy sidekick Tinker Bell, its power is entirely based on our collective belief in its existence.

Our conventional workweek was shaped by a period of rapid economic and technological change that concluded over a hundred years ago, during the industrial revolution. As we undergo another period of rapid disruption, we are once again in the unique position to reimagine how we work in a way that better suits today's needs.

———————————

Once upon a time, everyone worked from home, there was no separation between work and life, and our labor was very much in tune with nature. It is estimated that for ninety-five percent of human history, our species worked an average of fifteen hours per week. That work was typically fluid, flexible, and quintessentially human.[1]

For several thousand years before the industrial revolution, which began in the late 1700s, most of our stuff came from the ground and most of our labor was devoted to working that land. There were still some handmade goods and shops—like candlemakers, blacksmiths, shoe cobblers, and carpenters—but most of the things that were "manufactured" were crafted by individuals, by hand, one at a time.

That began to change in the early 1700s, when the British established what they called the *domestic system* of production—the sort of older, more laid-back cousin of the assembly line. While men worked the fields and tended to livestock, many women and children of the day—who also primarily resided in the countryside—worked as subcontractors for merchants in town. These subcontractors would receive a bundle of raw material, do some form of manual labor to turn it into a finished product (or something that better resembled one), and send it off to the next person in the chain of production. You can think of it like a home-based IKEA furniture building service; you get the parts and do the assembly on behalf of an anonymous end user.

In this example, IKEA doesn't have much of a reason to count how many hours you spend building furniture (or trying to find that one missing wooden peg that somehow keeps the whole thing from falling apart). All it cares about is how many Kiviks, Strandmons, Brimnes, and other hard-to-pronounce Swedish furniture items you assemble by the time it returns to haul away your finished goods to the store or the customer's home.

In the early industrial days, however, the most common application of this system was not affordable Scandinavian furniture, but textiles. Merchants typically sent bundles of wool to home-based subcontractors, who would use their at-home spinning wheels to spin them into yarn. Those familiar with the German fairy tale "Rumpelstiltskin," published by the Brothers Grimm in 1812, might recall the small, creepy stranger who offered to spin straw into gold in exchange for the future firstborn child of a miller's daughter. Aside from scaring German children, the unsettling tale also demonstrates how common it was for women of the day to spend their time toiling away at their spinning wheels. Once they finished spinning wool into yarn, these subcontractors sent the slightly more finished product to a handweaver, who would turn it into clothing or another textile product. This is where the term *cottage industry* comes from, since most of that day's labor was completed in rural cottages. Young women, who typically weren't enrolled in school or helping on the farm, spent most of their time engaged in this kind of work. Married women, however, were not expected to participate as frequently, instead spending most of their time tending to the home or their children. That is why some still (quite cruelly and unfairly) call unmarried women of a certain age *spinsters*.

Whether you worked in agriculture or in the early days of manufacturing, you probably worked alongside family, neighbors, and friends, on your own property and on nature's schedule. Your day didn't have an official start and end time, and nobody was watching the clock (or more likely, the sundial) to ensure you worked the correct number of hours. There were tasks that had to get done and rough deadlines for their completion set by natural cycles like sundown and seasons' change, but individuals were otherwise free to determine when and how to accomplish those tasks. In this environment, success was most dependent on the individual's most human skills, like creative problem-solving, resilience, adaptability, and a strong work ethic.

That was true for most of recorded human history, right up until about 250 years ago, when new technologies made both agriculture and manufacturing significantly more efficient and more reliant on heavy machinery than on human labor. In the late 1700s and early 1800s, new technologies like the steam engine, better plow technology, and more advanced farming equipment meant that people were able to do a lot more in less time, and with fewer workers. By the 1841 British census, just 22 percent of the country's workforce remained in the agriculture sector, which had been the primary focus of human labor for most of recorded history up to that point.[2] The sudden and rapid advancement of technology, and the workforce displacement that resulted, sent the world into a panic. People were petrified that the new machines would take away everyone's jobs (sound familiar?).

At that time, it was hard to imagine what people would do with themselves other than farming or some other cottage industry work, given that there had never been any other major form of employment in our species' history, other than hunter-gatherer. Of course, there were plenty of jobs created by the very same industrial revolution that eliminated most roles in agriculture, but it was nearly impossible to imagine a manufacturing sector that didn't yet exist and the countless jobs it would create. Now you can find charts that show a nearly perfect alignment between the loss of agricultural jobs and the rise of industrial labor. Though the transition of the economy was much less smooth in practice and many were left behind, it eventually became clear that as the old methods of production shed most of its workers, a new method of production was eager to scoop them up.

Work in a manufacturing facility, however, couldn't be much more different from work on a farm. To start, factories didn't exist in our backyards, which meant that for the first time in human history, people had to move away from the countryside to find work. In 1851, British census data revealed that more people were living in towns and cities than the countryside for the first time ever.[3]

But it wasn't just where people worked that got flipped on its head after the industrial revolution. During this period, so much of what had forever been casual, ad hoc, and self-regulated became measured, managed, and optimized for efficiency. Workers, for the first time, were paid by the hour, not according to their total output. They had a designated workstation where they would work alongside strangers and colleagues, not family and neighbors. They had managers and bosses and hierarchies watching over their shoulders, enforcing new rules, standards, and expectations. Most workers also went from managing a long list of daily tasks around the farm to doing a simple job—like twisting a screw or hammering a nail—repeatedly all day long. The era's major breakthrough, the assembly line, was in many ways designed to turn humans into robots doing menial, repetitive tasks over and over, with as little variation as possible.

At first, working conditions were incredibly harsh. As more people left the countryside to find opportunity in cities and towns, factory owners had little incentive to treat their workers with respect and dignity, knowing that those who complained could be easily replaced. Up until this point, humans thrived by leaning on their most human traits, but the industrialized world of work prized our most robotic ones. Creative problem-solving, adaptability, resourcefulness, and emotional intelligence had no place on the industrial-era factory floor. Instead, workers were valued for demonstrating traits like punctuality, loyalty, obedience, and consistency. During this period, workers were implicitly—and even explicitly—expected to check their humanity at the door and operate like a cog in the big industrial machine.

In the early industrial revolution, there were no evenings or weekends, no vacation days or sick days or parental leave. Those who showed up to work were paid for the hours they worked, and those who didn't were replaced. Factories only made money when they were operational, and factory owners were financially motivated to keep production running for as many hours as possible. At the beginning of the industrial revolution, workers might only get a few hours off per day to sleep before returning to work, seven days a week. A US government study from 1890, for example, found that full-time manufacturing employees worked an average of one hundred hours per week, or just over fourteen hours a day over seven days.[4] As recently as 150 years ago, concepts like paid vacation, sick leave, parental leave, or even weekends were entirely foreign or mere pipedreams.

Throughout this period, there were many efforts to make work a little more human, perhaps most notably the campaign to institute an eight-hour workday. That idea is credited to a Welsh manufacturer and labor rights activist named Robert Owen, who coined the phrase "eight hours labor, eight hours recreation, eight hours rest" all the way back in 1817.[5] At first, most rejected that notion, especially in Europe. Treating workers like humans was bad for business, and in the early nineteenth century, Western economies were still duking it out for manufacturing supremacy, leaving little appetite for slowing things down. The idea of splitting the day into three equal parts, however, was picked up by American labor rights activists after the Civil War. In 1866, the National Labor Union asked Congress to pass a law mandating the eight-hour workday, but to no avail. Three years later, President Ulysses S. Grant finally instituted the eight-hour workday, but it only applied to federal government workers.

Despite the effort's limited success in the political arena, however, private-sector employers in certain industries started to champion the cause—especially in industries that required specialized skills or benefited from our more human traits. The prevailing wisdom at the time was that factory workers didn't need time off to think, rest, or spend time with their families but that those in charge of making important decisions, thinking critically, or coming up with new ideas did. In fact, it was the printing industry—the primary mass media of the day—that first made the eight-hour workday standard for its workers, in around 1905.[6]

As the eight-hour workday gradually gained momentum in select corners of the economy, concurrent efforts to reduce the number of workdays in a week began to take shape. In the early nineteenth century, Christian Sabbatarians—followers of a religious movement organized around championing the fourth commandment, "Remember the Sabbath day, to keep it holy"—successfully lobbied the US government to close the post office on Sundays so that workers could attend church.[7] Over time, other employers followed suit, succumbing to both religious pressure and labor market competition. Jewish workers, meanwhile, were given Saturdays off to observe their weekly Sabbath and were commonly asked to make up their work on Sundays. Eventually, however, the religious majority grew offended that anyone, be they Christian or not, would go to work on Sundays. To settle the issue, a New England mill became what is believed to be the first factory to institute a five-day workweek, in 1908, to accommodate the Sabbaths of both major religions.[8] (To this day, many nations with non-Christian majority populations—including many Muslim and Jewish-majority countries in the Middle East—start their weekends on Thursday evening and return to work on Sunday morning.[9])

In the ensuing years, other factories dealing with the same pressure to ensure that nobody worked on what their staff considered the Lord's day moved to a five-day schedule as well, but the first of the "great American industrialists" to really champion the five-day workweek was Henry Ford. In 1922, he introduced a forty-hour workweek consisting of five eight-hour days on a trial basis.

At the time, the decision was seen as rather controversial and a major blow to American productivity. A 1922 *New York Herald* editorial, for example, suggested that "the Ford plan is joyous news to all who like to think of bringing work down to the irresistible minimum."[10] That's 1922 talk for "Ford is encouraging laziness." Ford, however, was in the business of selling cars, and in the early days of the automotive industry, workers had little use for a car if they didn't have time to drive it. Today we often associate driving with going to work, but back in the days before suburbs and major urban sprawl, cars were primarily used for longer trips to the countryside, while commuting to work typically involved a train, a bicycle, or just your feet.

"The industrial value of leisure as a promoter of the consumption of goods, and thus as a stimulant to business, have been proved," Ford wrote in 1926, the same year that his entire workforce permanently moved to a five-day workweek, which he offered along with a $5 per day minimum wage. "It is high time to rid ourselves of the notion that leisure for workmen is either 'lost time' or a class privilege."[11]

In other words, Ford recognized that only the wealthy were buying cars, because they were the only ones with enough disposable income and leisure time to justify purchasing one. If he wanted to expand the market for automobiles from the upper class to the masses, he'd need to encourage a system that gave factory workers adequate pay and time off. Of course, we all know how that worked out for Ford, but at the time he was considered a pariah in the American business community. (While we do acknowledge Ford's forward-thinking perspective on workplace issues, we must also recognize his reprehensible and well-documented history of extreme antisemitism and bigotry.[12])

Over the ensuing years, other employers followed suit, and by the time the Fair Labor Standards Act was amended to codify the forty-hour workweek in America in 1940—a mere eighty-six years ago—most employers were already operating on an eight-hour, five-day schedule. The ruling required employers to pay higher overtime rates starting on the forty-first hour, effectively encouraging them to limit worker schedules to forty, which most companies split into five days of eight hours, from Monday to Friday, for all the religious and political reasons outlined above. The legislation wasn't designed to establish new conventions but rather codified that which had already been widely adopted. By 1980, the hours of nine to five had become so universally adopted that Dolly Parton wrote a hit song and starred in a whole movie about it.

There were attempts to further reduce the workweek in the years that followed, but none were ultimately successful. In 1956, for example, then Vice President Richard Nixon promised a four-day workweek thanks to his administration's economic policies.[13]

"Back-breaking toil and mind-wearying tension will be left to machines and electronic devices," said Nixon during a campaign speech.[14] "We want man's work to be pleasant so that he can go home each day with abundant energy for enjoying the comfort and friendliness of his family. We see the time not too far distant when we can have a four-day week and family life will be even more fully enjoyed by every American." Roughly seventy years later, that "time not too far distant" has yet to arrive.

———————————

For many, the story ends there. For us, it's just the beginning.

Almost exactly one hundred years after Henry Ford standardized the forty-hour workweek and eighty-six years after it was signed into law, most of us still maintain a schedule designed to facilitate the transition from an agrarian to an industrialized economy. That is despite having since moved on to a very different world of work—one that again prizes our most human traits. Most workers are no longer simply valued for showing up on time, punching a clock, and doing the same menial task over and over again. Today, as was true for most of human history, our ability to survive and thrive depends largely on our most human traits—traits like creative problem-solving, adaptability, resourcefulness, and emotional intelligence. While strict oversight, control, and standardization were vital to the success of the economy in the days of the industrial revolution, most of us aren't working on an assembly line anymore, and even those who do have a dramatically different work experience than the factory workers of that era.

In our modern knowledge economy, many of the rules and norms that emerged during the industrial revolution to standardize physical labor aren't well positioned for our current reality, yet they remain firmly in place. That was, at least, until the Covid-19 pandemic gave us permission to reevaluate how work gets done, whether conventional rules like location and standard hours really matter in today's workplace, and what role work plays in our lives. Not long after that major disruption, the world caught its first glimpse of a powerful new technology, one that has the potential to dramatically increase our collective output, not unlike the tools introduced at the start of the industrial revolution.

Given the challenges that have resulted from the application of outdated workplace rules and norms to our modern reality (which we discuss in greater detail in the chapters ahead), and given the technological, societal, and economic disruptions that lie around the corner, we must again reimagine how work gets done.

If the establishment of the five-day workweek serves as a model, change will originate at the grassroots level, with everyday workers advocating for better conditions, armed with evidence that the change is better for business, the economy, and society at large. Next will come the business leaders, specifically the more forward-thinking ones or those operating in more specialized fields with more competitive talent markets. If history is any guide, laws and policies will only change *after* the private sector adopts new norms.

As with the last major adjustment to working hours, many people paint the four-day workweek as emblematic of a decline in work ethic or a rise in laziness of epidemic proportions. Having studied the issue closely, we disagree, and as the five-day advocates of the last century found, history will be on our side. As we undergo another seismic shift in how work is accomplished, as technology again plays an outsize role, history tells us that we have another once-in-a-century opportunity to set a new standard and rewrite the rules to better reflect our modern reality. As in the early nineteenth century, many companies are already experimenting with a shorter workweek, and research is starting to mount that it's not just viable but necessary.

Early manufacturing and agriculture were both maddeningly inefficient, there's no denying that. But in our pursuit of hyperproductivity, we lost many of the things that made work meaningful, manageable, and human. As more advanced technologies take over our most robotic tasks—thus increasing the value of our most human traits—we have an opportunity to get them back. We don't know about you, but we don't want to wait another hundred years for the next major advancement in how work is structured.

3 The Emergence of a Four-Day Alternative

In 2018, as director of Campaigns for Fórsa, Ireland's largest labor union for public sector workers, one of us (Joe O'Connor) led a research project analyzing work-life balance and working hours among the union's members.

In his research, Joe discovered that a significant proportion of working parents—primarily women—had shifted to a four-day schedule with an equivalent reduction in pay. When he dug a little deeper, however, he discovered that their job expectations and responsibilities had not declined in kind—nor had their performance.

In other words, they were accomplishing as much in four days as they had previously done in five. Another odd wrinkle of the public service world offered an additional unexpected insight. An austerity-era collective settlement known as the Haddington Road Agreement enforced an extra two hours and fifteen minutes of work on public servants each week. As he dug a little deeper, Joe discovered that the extra hours were not explicitly tied to extra productivity or higher expectations in most roles. For example, the health-care system experienced a quantifiable gain when nurses added a couple of extra hours to their shifts, but the same could not be said of the thousands of managers, administrators, and other support roles that were included in the policy—though it did prove a source of some bitterness among those members.

That's when Joe discovered Parkinson's law, a theory developed by naval historian C. Northcote Parkinson. In a 1955 essay published in the *Economist*, Parkinson tells the story of an "elderly lady of leisure" sending a postcard to her niece.[1] He explains that this simple task could fill this woman's entire day; an hour spent finding the perfect postcard, another hour "hunting for spectacles," a half hour looking up the address, an hour and a quarter writing the letter, and twenty minutes deciding whether to take an umbrella on her casual walk to the post office—a walk that may include browsing through a few shops along the way. "The total effort which would occupy a busy man for three minutes all told may in this fashion leave another person prostrate after a day of doubt, anxiety, and toil." That observation ultimately led Parkinson to conclude that "work expands so as to fill the time available for its completion." In other words, our "elderly lady of leisure" gave herself a full day to complete a task and used up the entirety of that time. If she was given the same time allotment as the "busy man," Parkinson believes she could have done the same task in three minutes.

A more modern example can be found in the American version of the hit British sitcom *The Office*. In an episode that aired in 2006, regional manager Michael Scott hosts Movie Mondays in the office.[2] After his superior from corporate, Jan Levinson, walks in on the entire staff watching a movie during working hours in the break room, she demands an explanation as to how a movie could boost productivity, to which Michael responds, "People work faster after."

"Magically?" Jan asks.

"No," Michael responds, "they have to, to make up for the time they lost watching a movie."

While Jan may be unimpressed, the exchange demonstrates how most workplaces could find a few extra hours in the day or week if they had to, while still getting all their work done.

Parkinson's law speaks to the same concept that jumped out at Joe from the labor union productivity data. When workers were given thirty-five hours to complete a task, they got it done in thirty-five. When their schedules were extended to thirty-seven hours, most accomplished the same. And when they were asked to do the same task in thirty-two hours, they adjusted their processes accordingly and got the same amount of work done in less time.

As part of his duties with the trade union—and as its youngest assistant general secretary—Joe was tasked with addressing low engagement and unionization rates among young workers in Ireland. Around the same time, he had been following some emerging trials in places like Sweden, Iceland, and New Zealand in the mid-to-late-2010s, where early pilots of a four-day workweek showed promising results. Joe believed that the same experiment could work in his native country, but the problem was that nobody really took the shorter workweek seriously. Even today, sitting on a mountain of research, evidence, and real-world case studies, we often hear things like "But really, you don't actually think it could work, do you?" So you can imagine how the idea was received back then. Fortunately, Joe is the kind of guy who gets inspired by his doubters, and he only grew more confident that the four-day workweek occupied the perfect slice in the middle of the Venn diagram between ambitious and achievable.

In 2018 he hosted a conference in Dublin called The Future of Working Time, bringing together international speakers and experts on the subject. It was there that Joe's then boss Kevin Callinan declared his objective of winning a four-day week for the union's membership within a decade, an effort that remains ongoing. Even then, Joe found himself talking about the potential of advancements in technology to increase our productive capacity in the future, recognizing how work time and compensation had hardly budged in the last half century, despite significant technologically driven productivity gains. "We believe that we should be talking about productivity rather than time," he told local media in 2018. "When you look at the technological changes that are coming down the line—the fourth industrial revolution of artificial intelligence, automation—it's vitally important that the benefits from that are shared with workers."[3]

Theories about the four-day workweek at the time, however, were largely just that—theories. While some individual companies and employees had found success working on a reduced schedule, there had yet to be a major formal coordinated study on the subject, and Joe was eager to change that.

The following year, in 2019, Joe launched the Four Day Week Ireland campaign and began reaching out to the small but passionate group of international business leaders who had taken up the cause. Among them was a man named Andrew Barnes, who had successfully implemented the shorter schedule at his estate planning company, Perpetual Guardian, in New Zealand. Around that time Andrew and his spouse, Charlotte Lockhart, launched 4 Day Week Global to help formalize the study of the shorter workweek, and the new organization was eager to support Joe's ambitions to set up a trial in Ireland.

In late 2020, Joe recruited twelve small Irish businesses that were willing to make the switch, and brought in research partners from Boston College and University College Dublin to study the results. Among them was Juliet Schor, an internationally recognized economist and sociologist. Schor had been studying and writing about the relationship between work and time for decades, as exemplified in her 1991 bestselling book *The Overworked American*.[4] The research initiative not only added some extra credibility to the project but also established a foundation for the growing body of research that sought to quantify the impact of a four-day workweek on participating businesses, employees, and society at large. The research also made great fodder for the master's thesis Joe had deferred when he had assumed a series of leadership roles at Atlantic Technological

University's Students' Union, as president of the Union of Students in Ireland, and, eventually, with Fórsa.

In 2021, Joe kicked off the world's first coordinated four-day work-week trial in Ireland and followed it up with another that included twenty-one companies in the United States and Canada the next year. With each pilot, Joe was seeing more promising results. Around this time, he took on a one-year visiting research fellowship at Cornell University to study the concept further and, soon after, took over as 4 Day Week Global's CEO. In this role, he coordinated the organization's pilot programs in the United States, Canada, the United Kingdom, Australia, and New Zealand using the model he had developed in Ireland. If you've read anything about the four-day workweek in the past, there's a good chance it cited one or more of these studies.

While the pandemic had initially caused some added complications—making it hard to compare data against a neutral baseline, given how much all businesses were evolving during that time—it also offered a unique opportunity. As organizations took the challenges of the pandemic as a chance to reevaluate some of their long-standing workplace practices, there was a heightened degree of open-mindedness to doing things differently. Employees, meanwhile, were struggling under the weight of the many strains the pandemic brought when they found themselves in an historically competitive labor market. Suddenly, workers also felt empowered to question long-standing workplace norms and to demand big-ticket items that would have previously been considered nonstarters. In 2019, requesting a remote job or hybrid role seemed like a radical request; by 2021, it had become standard, leading some to wonder what other workplace norms might be less permanent than previously thought.

––––––––––

Through each successful pilot program, Joe's initial hypothesis—that workers can really do as much, or more, in less time under the right circumstances—proved true. What he hadn't expected to find, however, was the diversity of companies interested in pursuing a four-day workweek and the diversity of workers, industries, and roles that were able to make the switch successfully.

During that time, Joe worked with companies big and small, domestic and global, independent and corporate owned, public and private sector, knowledge-based and industrial, unionized and non-union. He met B Corp founders who saw the four-day workweek as a tool to reduce emissions and law firms that saw the four-day workweek as a tool to reduce burnout. He worked with agencies and tech companies that used it to recruit the industry's best and brightest in a highly competitive talent market and union organizers who used it to find middle ground with cash-strapped employers. Politicians on the left saw the four-day workweek as an imperative for workers in an increasingly unfair economy, and politicians on the right saw it as a matter of individual liberty and fiscal responsibility. (We will meet some of those business and political leaders in the chapters ahead.)

All the while, Joe was working with top-tier research institutions to demonstrate results, which began making regular appearances in news outlets around the world. The world's largest pilot, which included sixty-one UK-based companies and their more than three thousand employees, made global headlines after nearly every participating organization said they intended to make the switch permanent. Nearly half also said their productivity improved, including 15 percent that said it "improved significantly," while 46 percent reported that productivity remained the same, and just 5 percent said it declined.[5]

That study was quickly followed by a similar trial in North America, where the forty-one participating employers logged an average boost in revenue of 15 percent over the twelve-month term, despite reducing working hours. Workers who participated in the trial ranked the experience a 9.1 out of 10, with the vast majority saying they would like the four-day workweek to be made permanent. Every participating organization decided to retain the four-day structure after the trial. The researchers also concluded that stress, fatigue, and work-life conflict had all declined among the participants, while physical health, mental health, sleep hours, work-life balance, and general life satisfaction all increased significantly. The shorter work-week enabled male participants to spend more time with their families and encouraged them to chip in more at home, better balancing the scales of unpaid domestic labor (more on that later).[6] Even those who did some work on their days off said that they were more focused and productive, simply by making the hours that were once mandatory entirely optional.

Joe long understood that the four-day workweek was not only viable but also beneficial to a wide range of companies and workers. Through his work over the last eight years, he's now got the receipts to prove it. In 2022, he cofounded Work Time Revolution, a global consulting and research firm that specializes in building new models of work that reduce overwork, support employee wellbeing, promote sustainable performance, and drive organizational effectiveness. There, he partners with organizations to help teams and individuals achieve more while working less.

———————

Early on, Joe learned that the four-day workweek inspires great passion—and with it, media attention—both positive and negative. As Henry Ford and Robert Owens learned long ago, telling people they can do more while working fewer hours doesn't always go over well with certain audiences.

One of us (Jared Lindzon) was one of the reporters who saw the potential of a shorter workweek early on and began writing about it in 2020. Like Joe, Jared had witnessed the gap between output and hours in his own work long before arriving at the four-day workweek as a solution. As a freelance journalist, Jared operates what is legally classified as a small business, balancing multiple assignments and clients at the same time, but the commodity he's selling is not widgets or hours but words. If Jared's rate is $1 per word, then a 500-word article comes with a price tag of $500 and a 5,000-word essay comes with a price tag of $5,000. That doesn't mean that his writing must be exactly the number of words he's being compensated for; it's industry standard that the work he submits is within 10 percent of the agreed-upon word count. That means a 500-word article will be somewhere between 450 and 550 words long. Measuring output in words instead of hours incentivizes Jared to work more efficiently; the more words he writes in a day, the more money he makes. If he uses new tools and technologies, better processes, and his own experience as a seasoned writer to do a lot more in less time, his earnings have a direct positive impact.

That assumption has actually proven true throughout his career; Jared earns much more today than he did ten years ago, despite little if any change to per-word rates, because the 500-word article that used to take him eight hours can typically be completed in two. That said, if he submits sloppy work as quickly as he can, he'll probably have to spend hours working with editors to bring it up to their standards. If it happens too often, he could risk losing a client. As a result, this compensation structure encourages efficiency as long as it doesn't come at the cost of quality.

If Jared were instead paid by the hour, he would have little reason to move quickly. In fact, he'd earn more money by taking more time to complete assignments. At the business-owner level—including businesses of one—figuring out creative ways to do things better, cheaper, and faster is rewarded with higher earnings and more leisure time.

Jared saw a clear and obvious opportunity for everyone else to use new tools and processes to achieve the same or more in less time, because he had already done so himself. As it stands today, however, the opposite is true for most employees; figuring out how to do things better, cheaper, and faster will probably result in being assigned more work. You might even risk having your employer question the necessity of your role. On meeting and interviewing Joe, Jared recognized how the four-day workweek could drive significant efficiencies by simply adopting an incentive structure that was already familiar to him.

Jared followed up his first story about the four-day workweek (published in the *Globe and Mail* in early 2020) with another a couple of years later, and he published two more in *Fast Company* in 2023. In the meantime, Joe had moved to Toronto to establish Work Time Revolution, and we finally met in person backstage at a tech conference in September 2022. Jared, serving as MC, introduced Joe to the crowd gathered at the event's "future of work" stage. By the time Jared had published his fifth story about the four-day workweek—a profile of Joe in the *Toronto Star* in early 2024—the pair decided it was time to collaborate on a book.

When Joe began studying the four-day workweek, he was one of just a handful of voices shouting its merits from the rooftops. Now, thanks in no small part to his efforts, he is joined by a chorus of advocates, business leaders, politicians, and individual workers who have come to the same conclusions.

These days you can find businesses operating on a four-day schedule in just about every major industry and in every major economy. Those who work in Lamborghini's production facilities, for example, switched to a four-day workweek in late 2023.[7] "The motivation of all the people in the organisation is the prime mover of its success because it calls together the best energies and skills of people around a common purpose," said the company's Chief People, Cultura and Organization Officer, Umberto Tossini. "The innovations introduced meet people's expectations through working hours that allow everyone to recover the physical and mental energies necessary for communal well-being."[8]

Unilever, which owns an exhaustive list of common household brands—including Dove, Degree, Hellmann's, Q-tips, St. Ives, TRESemmé, Vim, and Vaseline, to name just a few—switched its New Zealand and Australian teams to a four-day schedule after the pandemic and hasn't switched back (more on that in chapter 8). When

Microsoft Japan introduced a four-day workweek in 2019, productivity jumped 40 percent.[9] Buffer, Kickstarter, Grant Thornton, Bolt, and Awin also occupy spots on a growing list that now includes thousands of businesses operating on a shorter schedule. In fact, according to a study published by BrightHR in May 2024, there was a 25 percent jump in the number of UK businesses and a 34 percent jump among Canadian businesses that had adopted a four-day workweek in the twelve months prior.[10] In a 2025 study by Tech.co, 38 percent of senior leaders said they were open-minded about implementing a four-day workweek, compared with 23 percent the previous year.[11]

We aren't claiming that the four-day workweek universally delivers superior outcomes, just as few would argue that remote work is inherently better for every organization. However, much like remote work, it probably works for more people than previously assumed.

That includes those that work fully remote, those that are hybrid, and those that operate in-person; those that are currently in the business of selling hours, like lawyers and consultants, and those with high client demands; those that are bound by union contracts, and those that are not unionized; those that work at a desk, and those that work in the field; those that work for themselves, and those that work alongside thousands.

Like remote work, a four-day workweek must be designed and implemented thoughtfully to succeed. Those organizations and individuals that try to simply flip the switch—to cancel one day of the workweek without any planning or onboarding new tools and ways of working—are likely to fail, while those that first engage in the appropriate degree of planning and strategizing can achieve incredible results. As with remote work, the four-day workweek can reinforce positive work habits or further exacerbate underlying issues.

We acknowledge that—like remote work—organizations and people already maintaining a standard Monday-to-Friday, nine-to-five schedule, those in more knowledge-based industries, and those in more Westernized working cultures are likely to have an easier time making the transition.

At the same time—as was the case for remote work—we have seen organizations of all shapes and sizes and in a wide array of industries, geographical locations, and work cultures successfully make the switch even if it requires more energy and ingenuity at the outset. Not every organization is ready to become a four-day organization, at least not yet, but more can—and do—make the switch every year. No matter when you pick up this book, there will be more organizations working on a reduced schedule than there were last year, and there will be more next year. We believe this pattern will continue until there's a tipping point, when—like remote work—the four-day workweek becomes a competitive necessity for employers in certain fields and a popular solution for businesses seeking specific outcomes in others.

It sounds counterintuitive at first—reducing the workweek while maintaining or improving organizational outcomes—but once you dig into the details, it starts to make sense.

In purely mathematical terms, a four-day workweek is far less than a 20 percent reduction in work time once you factor in a sharp decline in absenteeism, sick leave, work-life conflicts, and turnover and essentially negate time off for statutory holidays (most four-day companies maintain a four-day schedule on holiday weeks, rather than three) and vacations (many four-day companies maintain the same number of vacation weeks but reduce the number of total days).

For employees, research suggests you can get a lot more done in less time when you are energized, well rested, more engaged in your work, and less distracted by personal responsibilities. The same is true of those who are more open to using new tools and practices and who put in the necessary work to develop new approaches to things like meetings and time management.

Like the five-day workweek or the eight-hour workday, what started off as something widely regarded as an outlandish idea has begun gaining traction among private-sector employers, inspiring a growing grassroots movement of everyday workers looking to build on that momentum. As with those earlier changes to standard operating hours, there is also a concurrent effort taking shape among the political class.

On March 13, 2024, independent Vermont senator and former Democratic presidential nominee Bernie Sanders introduced a bill to amend the Fair Labor Standards Act to start overtime compensation at thirty-two hours instead of the current forty, effectively signing the four-day workweek into law. In Senator Sanders's Thirty-Two Hour Workweek Act, he argues that American workers are now over 400 percent more productive than they were in 1940, when the five-day standard was set by Congress.[12] He points out that despite a massive increase in productivity, average wages are lower than they were fifty years ago, once adjusted for inflation. The act even cites the pilots led by Joe, noting that workers were more productive and less burned-out after making the switch, while businesses saw revenues increase. "These studies have also found reduced workweeks result in lower childcare costs and reduced carbon emissions," it argues.

Though the bill made global headlines, it was far from the first attempt at mandating a four-day workweek at the national level in the United States or in a major Western economy or in the modern era. In fact, such attempts have come from political bodies of all shapes and sizes around the world and across the political spectrum. In recent years, national efforts to implement a four-day workweek were initiated in Spain, Portugal, Scotland, Iceland, Lithuania, Poland, and the United Arab Emirates, with many of those efforts still ongoing.

In May of 2025 the Spanish Government passed a bill limiting public sector workers to 37.5 hours per week, down from the previous 40, and put forward another proposal to extend the reduced schedule to the private sector. "We are modernizing the world of labor and helping people to be a little happier," said Labor Minister Yolanda Díaz.[13]

In August 2008, the Republican governor of Utah, Jon Huntsman, reduced state employees' schedule to four days to address a budget shortfall. Government workers were asked to work four days of ten hours, allowing the state to close its offices on Fridays to help save on overhead. According to one study, Utah saved about $5.5 million during the first year of the experiment, including a $4 million reduction in overtime costs, without experiencing any decline in overall output.[14] It wasn't until Huntsman was voted out of office, in 2009, that his successor, Governor Gary Herbert, reversed the policy.

The Utah experiment, however, was just one of many promising political efforts to mandate a four-day week at the state and local level. As of mid-2025, state-level proposals had been filed by Democratic and Republican representatives in California, Maine, Maryland, Massachusetts, Missouri, New York, Pennsylvania, and Texas. Outside of the United States, small and local government-backed studies and pilot programs have been introduced in Japan, Korea, Sweden, and the United Kingdom.

If history is any guide, however, the political class will probably be the last to institute a four-day workweek, amending laws only after the practice has already been adopted by most private-sector employers. Remember, the eight-hour workday began as a grassroots movement—first in the United Kingdom and then in the United States—and then became a private-sector norm long before it was codified into the Fair Labor Standards Act in 1940. Even President Ulysses S. Grant, who believed in the merits of the eight-hour workday, was only able to institute it among federal workers. The five-day standard similarly began as a grassroots cause of the labor movement, and while it was eventually adopted by the US post office in 1905, it wasn't until 1940—fifteen years after Ford switched his production facilities to a five-day schedule—that the forty-hour workweek was signed into law.

Although these political efforts help bring attention and credibility to the four-day workweek, change is most likely to originate in academic papers, picket lines, break room chats, and Slack channels long before the conversation is brought into the boardroom and even longer before it reaches the Senate floor. When it comes to setting a new standard for working hours, history has proven that leaders, business owners and employees have more power to influence lasting change than their politicians. The future of the workweek isn't up to them; it's up to you.

4 AI and the Future of the Workweek

The technologies introduced during the industrial revolution dramatically changed the way we work, prompting society to reorganize itself around a new, more efficient way of getting things done.

Now, as the world prepares for the next revolutionary technology, the time has come for another major adjustment, one that is optimized for today's realities and tomorrow's challenges, not yesterday's norms. The five-day, eight-hour standard that carried us through the last century is not necessarily the best structure for our rapidly approaching AI future.

In fact, some of today's most influential business leaders have publicly declared the opportunity for AI to facilitate a shorter workweek. JPMorgan Chase CEO Jamie Dimon, for example, told Bloomberg TV reporters that their children will "probably be working three and a half days a week," thanks to the advancements in technology.[1] The billionaire owner of the New York Mets, Steve Cohen, is so confident that "a four-day workweek is coming" that in early 2024 he invested billions into leisure sports like golf, believing there would be greater demand in the future.[2] In September 2024, Zoom cofounder and CEO Eric Yuan told the audience at the Concordia Summit in New York that "very soon, maybe in the next 20 years or maybe sooner, we won't need to work for five days," adding that a four-day workweek "will become reality" as a direct result of advancements in AI technology.[3]

During a 2023 appearance on former *Daily Show* host Trevor Noah's podcast, Microsoft founder Bill Gates suggested that, thanks to AI, "you eventually get a society where you only have to work three days a week."[4] In early 2025, Jared got the opportunity to ask the billionaire philanthropist about it further. Specifically, he wanted to know why Gates believed the impact of AI on working hours would be any different from the other productivity-boosting technologies that came before it—many of which were developed by Gates and his team at Microsoft. "I do think AI is utterly different than previous innovations because it can be a substitute for human capability, as opposed to just an improvement in productivity," he told Jared remotely from his office near Palm Springs, California—over Microsoft Teams, of course. "This is going to reshape our world, not two generations from now, but within the current generation. Are we ready for that? And what does it mean for work?"[5]

Gates adds that he had just recently had dinner with a group of economists who were starting to bring those very questions to the highest levels of the US government. He adds that they were focused on ensuring that the productivity gains promised by AI are better shared than other recent innovations. "If you spread it around, you know, we're supposed to be better off," he says.

He adds that the technology offers societies an opportunity to reevaluate how work factors into individuals' lives and notes that Americans have historically chosen trade-offs that differed from Europeans' choices when it comes to work and leisure time. "Work plays such an important role in terms of 'That's why I get educated and develop predictable skills,' that it's almost the centering element of society," he says. "If we need a lot less of that, does some of that stuff about universal income—which is, you know, not affordable today, because we do need productive work for most of society to maintain this living standard—but once you have AI robots, it's a very, very different world, and I think people will choose to work less than they do today."

Gates's response prompted us to reach out to former Democratic presidential candidate Andrew Yang, with whom Jared had previously appeared on a panel. Yang made waves during his 2020 presidential run for championing universal basic income, or UBI, which gives every member of society a certain monthly sum to help cover basic living expenses. "I first heard about the efforts to reduce the workweek back in 2019," he tells us via email. "I felt it was a natural fit with the fact that technology was going to reduce the need and value of many workers."[6]

The tech entrepreneur turned politician tells us that he felt the two efforts—UBI and the four-day workweek—were complementary, as both sought to answer the same questions about the future of work in the age of AI. "The question is, 'what will we do when artificial intelligence makes our work increasingly irrelevant?'" Yang asks. "There will be growing pressure to reduce the number of workers in many roles and organizations, and shifting to a four-day workweek would preserve jobs at the margins."

While some fear that the four-day workweek will become a partisan issue—like everything else in Washington—Yang is confident that it can instead be a unifying cause for Americans of all political stripes. "I think there's a great chance that this is nonpartisan, because everyone wants a shorter workweek and it would make intuitive sense to most people," he wrote.

———

Since the deployment of ChatGPT in late 2022, economists, business leaders, academics, and politicians have drawn a direct line between AI and the need for a shorter workweek, and we're already starting to see that connection forming.

Although the technology remains in relative infancy, research shows that early adopters of AI are also more likely to be early adopters of the four-day workweek. According to a survey of one thousand American business leaders by London-based Tech.co, 29 percent of organizations that operate on a four-day schedule use AI extensively in their operations, compared with just 8 percent of those on a traditional five-day schedule.[7] Furthermore, 93 percent of organizations currently utilizing AI say they are open to a four-day workweek, compared with less than half of those that don't.

As mentioned previously, reducing the workweek without compromising outcomes requires finding ways to get things done more efficiently, and AI offers an effective way to do more in less time. A survey of three thousand employees in the United Kingdom, the United States, Canada, and Germany conducted by Visier found that those who utilized AI tools in the workplace saved 390 hours of working time per year, equivalent to 7.5 hours per workweek, or about one full workday.[8] In the time since the survey was conducted, in May 2023, the technology has advanced significantly. In other words, AI is already giving workers one extra day's worth of efficiency, and it's only just the beginning.

Another study, conducted later that same year by Autonomy Institute, suggests that 71 percent of the US labor market, or about 128 million workers, could reduce their working hours by 10 percent within a decade without losing any productivity, simply by adopting AI technologies built on large language models.[9] A follow-up study, wherein Joe and his team at Work Time Revolution collaborated with Autonomy, found the same results for 90 percent of Canadian workers.[10] Organizations that adopt both approaches—AI and a four-day workweek—at the same time often see the productivity gains of the former more than make up for any losses caused by the latter. They also tend to have more success in their adoption efforts, because the four-day workweek has proven itself a powerful incentive for technological adoption and broader organizational transformation.

According to a 2024 report by the RAND Corporation estimated that more than 80 percent of AI projects fail—double the failure rate of information technology projects that don't involve AI.[11] While many of the common failure points are technological, the most common cause is misalignment, misunderstanding, and miscommunications with stakeholders. In a 2025 survey of 2,000 executives in thirteen countries by the Adecco Group, just one in ten said they are "future-ready" when it comes to the leadership alignment, talent strategy, and internal skills needed to adopt AI responsibly. In fact, leaders reported ten percent *lower* levels of confidence in their AI strategies than in the same survey one year prior.[12]

In the European Commission's Generative AI Outlook report, which published in June of 2025, 85 percent of enterprises said AI was a strategic priority. However, fewer than 20 percent had redesigned work to support its adoption, and just 11 percent of employees said they have received guidance for using AI tools, citing a lack of available time as their primary barrier.[13]

According to a 2025 study by Writer, a generative AI platform, 31 percent of employees admit to "sabotaging" their company's AI strategy, typically by refusing to adopt new tools or by not participating in efforts to assist their integration.[14] As a result, two-thirds of executives surveyed say AI adoption is a source of tension and division in their organizations, and 42 percent say its "tearing their company apart." A 2025 study by global IT service provider Kyndryl similarly found that among CEOs 45 percent believe most employees are resistant or even hostile toward AI.[15]

Leaders' instincts are telling them that their people aren't ready, willing, and eager to adopt new AI tools, and the data suggests they're right. A 2023 study by Leadership IQ found that just 10 percent of staff were "excited" about AI adoption, and another 35 percent are "cautiously optimistic," while the remainder said they were indifferent, reluctant, or outright resistant.[16] When the study was repeated in early 2025, the answers were almost identical.[17] While more workers had moved from having "no experience" with AI to "beginner," Leadership IQ founder and CEO Mark Murphy says many continue to resist. "The numbers are looking mildly better, but not drastically. There was still a shocking amount of denial," he told Jared in an interview for *Fast Company* in March 2025. "We're still playing with it as a one-off tool—something we depart from our normal job and play with for a few minutes, have it answer a question or two, rather than fully integrating it into our work."[18] Without some kind of incentive, the data suggests most businesses will face resistance to adopting the technologies that will become a competitive differentiator in the near future.

The studies illustrate another important consideration about the rapid advancement of the world's most powerful technology. The data suggests that people are often afraid to modernize their work processes, and in recent years, they have been given plenty of reasons to be resistant. When business leaders pursue a major overhaul of their operations, it is the lower-level workers and managers who are largely responsible for doing the hard work of implementing that change on the ground. They are also typically those who benefit the least from it. Sure, the company might provide greater job security as it becomes more competitive, and perhaps those efforts will pay off in some future promotion or salary increase, if they're lucky. For most frontline staff, however, technological adoption is something that makes their jobs more difficult in the short term and less secure in the long run while primarily enriching their corporate leaders and shareholders. It's a pattern that has been instilled over generations; as corporations enjoy record profits, the standard of living for the rest has hardly budged, and many of our most sacred institutions are crumbling. In the last few decades mobile technology, cloud computing, and social media have made businesses more efficient, profitable, and agile while making individuals more isolated, angry, and afraid. No wonder so many are so actively resistant to change.

In a 1930 essay titled "Economic Possibilities for Our Grandchildren," British economist and philosopher John Maynard Keynes predicted that technology would usher in an "age of leisure and abundance without dread." With our "new-found bounty," we would all be free to "map out for ourselves a plan of life," effectively making traditional work mostly voluntary.[19]

"Everybody will need to do some work if he is to be contented," Keynes wrote. "We shall do more things for ourselves than is usual with the rich today, only too glad to have small duties and tasks and routines. . . . Three-hour shifts or a fifteen-hour week may put off the problem for a great while." In the late days of the industrial revolution, economists like Keynes were certain that the rapid advancements in technology and the quality-of-life improvements they witnessed in their own lifetimes would eventually result in a world where everyone lived like the aristocracy of the day, engaging in work to satisfy personal ambitions rather than out of economic necessity.

Since then, not only has technology advanced beyond Keynes's wildest imagination, but so has workforce participation. At that time, less than 20 percent of American women worked outside the home, and the US population was about one-third of what it is today. That means there has been a massive explosion in not just the productivity of individual workers and the proportion of the population engaged in the workforce but the sheer number of people participating in the US economy. So why aren't we all living like aristocrats? Because most of the benefits of that advancement have flowed upward.

After all, it doesn't take a lot of study and analysis to recognize that you can get a lot more done in a day using a smartphone and laptop than a fax machine and an abacus, or a pencil and a legal pad. But the benefits of these leaps in personal productivity have not been matched with increases in pay or time off from work. According to the Economic Policy Institute, between 1948 and 1973—during the dawn of the computing age—a 97 percent jump in individual productivity was coupled with an inflation-adjusted 91.3 percent increase in average hourly wages.[20] During the early internet age between 1973 and 2013, however, productivity increased by another 74 percent while average hourly compensation increased by just 9 percent once adjusted for inflation. Workers were indeed getting more productive, thanks to significant advancements in technology, yet they rarely benefited from those gains. In fact, workers in the age of smartphones, cloud computing, and broadband internet are still working the same hours as those who were around during the invention of the light bulb and are getting paid about the same as those who were around before the invention of the personal computer.

"Why would it be different for AI?" asks Nobel Prize–winning economist Christopher Pissarides. Sir Christopher—who was knighted by Queen Elizabeth II in 2013 and has asked that we not call him by his formal name, but we couldn't resist—made global headlines in April 2023, and again that December, for announcing, then reaffirming, his belief that AI will usher in a four-day workweek in the coming years.[21] Speaking to us from his home in England, the London School of Economics professor explains that he made his headline-grabbing declaration after the public release of OpenAI's ChatGPT. That, he says, gave the world a glimpse into just how far AI had come in recent years and a sense of what the future may hold.

"If it's left completely unregulated, AI is going to give rise to even bigger inequalities than previous technologies," he says.[22] Sir Christopher explains that previous waves of technology only furthered the gap between the haves and the have-nots, hollowing out the middle class. As more workers feel left behind by these advancements, they're losing faith in once-trusted institutions. The result is our current state of heightened social division. Advancements in robotics, for example, made manufacturing cheaper and manufacturing companies more profitable while eliminating countless middle-class, low-skill jobs. "Now AI is having the same impact, so we need to regulate it if everyone is going to benefit," he says. "If you're not going to pay workers more, and yet they're contributing so much more to your productivity [thanks to AI], then you might as well give them some more time off."

Sir Christopher—like Bill Gates—believes the proliferation of AI will be different from the productivity-boosting technologies that came before. Unlike previous waves of innovation, new AI tools are becoming widely available at reasonable price points and with relatively minimal barriers to entry. For example, you don't need to know how to code or hire a team of engineers to enjoy the productivity benefits of AI technologies. Despite the minimal costs to individuals, the potential upside is massive, especially for knowledge workers. "The new technologies we're discovering are really much more complementary, much more favorable to highly skilled workers, rather than the unskilled," Sir Christopher says. "At the more general level, AI enables us to organize work in different ways, including remote working, including postponing things—doing them in our own time, because everything will be recorded—and it's thought that there will be productivity gains. So if you're going to be able to organize your work in a flexible way, and if there are going to be productivity gains, then it makes it a lot easier to pack everything into four days and not lose any income, because you will become more productive with the new technology." Proof of that exact dynamic came minutes after our meeting, when Sir Christopher was provided an AI-produced summary of the call, along with a transcript and video, all of which were auto-generated by a service that costs $8 per month.

In a world where affordable, broadly available technology can assist with countless workplace tasks the individuals and organizations that succeed will be those that work smarter, not longer.

When we talk about AI, we should acknowledge that most people still associate the technology with widespread job displacement.

If the doomers and gloomers are right, AI will usher in a world where most will be happy to get any work they can. But we think those predictions are unlikely to come to fruition. Instead of workforce displacement, most experts on the subject believe AI will usher in a workforce pivot, rendering some jobs obsolete while giving rise to roles and industries we can't yet imagine. Remember, people in the early nineteenth century panicked when new technologies started to displace workers in the world's largest industry, agriculture, because they couldn't have possibly imagined the jobs that would be created in the future. After all, it would be pretty hard to explain to a farmer in those days that their children would have plenty of job opportunities in the automotive sector, before the invention of the automobile. As with that period of rapid economic change, it's similarly impossible for us to know what kinds of jobs AI will create. But rest assured, there will be room for human labor.

However, just as the industrial revolution changed the kinds of skills we needed to thrive in that economy—specifically, from our most human traits to our most robotic ones—AI is poised to have an equally dramatic (albeit opposite) effect. When powerful machines can do repetitive work that prescribes to a formula, there will be a greater need for humanity to demonstrate its ability to think outside the box, to hone our creativity, problem-solving, critical thinking, and other inherently human traits.

Once upon a time, accountants spent most of their time doing mathematical equations in a backroom by hand. Organizations needed teams of bean counters to do basic arithmetic and to check each other's work, but the role was considered more in the realm of grunt work than the stuff of corporate leadership. Though they worked with pen and paper, the accounting profession was intentionally designed to mimic the assembly lines of industrial-era factories. Until the 1960s, electric calculators cost more than a team of human accountants and required about as much physical office space.[23] The first electronic desktop calculator, ANITA (which stands for A New Inspiration To Arithmetic/Accounting), hit the market in 1961 and sold for about $1,000 (or about $10,500 in today's dollars).[24] By the end of the decade, technology manufacturers like Sharp, Canon, Sanyo, and Texas Instruments introduced a range of portable calculators, which came in closer to $2,000 in today's money. By the mid-1970s, numerous competitors in the United States, the United Kingdom, the Soviet Union, and Japan entered the market, offering calculators designed for professionals as well as some priced low enough for everyday users. Today, you can buy a calculator that fits on a watch for $30. So why do we still have accountants?

If the primary function of the accounting profession was to crunch numbers, then a machine that could do that task with a higher degree of accuracy in a fraction of the time should have wiped that industry out entirely. Instead, as the affordability and availability of calculators skyrocketed, so did the number of accountants in the United States. In 1960, before the proliferation of the calculator, the "Big Eight" American accounting firms employed 1,071 accountants; by 1981, they collectively employed more than 7,000.[25] Today there are more than 1.56 million accounting and auditing professionals in the United States, with an estimated annual employment growth of 6 percent. Even though just about everyone now has a powerful calculator in their pocket, the job market for accountants and auditors is expected to grow faster than national averages over the next decade, according to the Bureau of Labor Statistics.[26]

Today the accounting profession has been elevated from backroom bean counters to chief financial officers, often one step removed from the highest position in the organization. In fact, these days it's quite common for CEOs themselves to rise out of the accounting discipline. A 2019 study of the *Fortune* 100 found that 22 percent of the world's top CEOs began their careers in finance, the second-most-popular pathway after operations.[27] Rather than rendering accounting positions obsolete, the widespread availability of calculators has allowed accountants to ditch the low-level number crunching and add entirely new kinds of value to the organization.

Their rise from the backroom to the executive suite also had a significant impact on the skills required to be an effective accounting professional. Today you can't make it to the highest levels of the profession simply for being good at math. Accountants are instead required to use the tools at their disposal—including the calculator, spreadsheets, AI, and countless other more complex types of software—to act in more of a high-level advisory and leadership role. Managing billings, receivables, compliance, and audits is the baseline; now accountants are also in the business of forecasting, financial modeling, market analysis, and investing.

In other words, technology that was once predicted to eliminate the role has instead transformed the kinds of skills necessary to succeed, from the more robotic traits to more human skills—like critical thinking—while elevating the value of the position itself. If this transformation happened to accountants, why can't it also happen to other technical roles that are poised to be disrupted by the upcoming wave of AI innovation?

Yes, AI's impact will be technological, and in terms of pure output, it will increase our capacity to do more in less time, but that's just the beginning. AI is also poised to usher in dramatic changes to the economy, the labor market, the social contract between employers and employees, and the role work plays in our lives. Up until recently, the dramatic leaps in innovation have had little impact on the average person's wealth or quality of life. As we enter the age of AI, we have a unique opportunity to change the narrative, to use the gains promised by technology to improve living standards and to help restore our faith in our institutions and each other.

5 Redefining Productivity

Measuring productivity in terms of output over hours is a long-outdated vestige of the industrial revolution but one that has proven incredibly difficult to evolve beyond. While this approach causes numerous challenges and conflicts in the workplace, there is surprisingly little appetite to change it.

That is because hours have the undeniable benefit of being universal. When we talk about output, compensation, or expectations, time worked provides a convenient and broadly understood measurement tool. Whether you're a baker in Manila, a banker on Wall Street, or a cocoa farmer in Nigeria, those sixty minutes mean the exact same thing and are measured in the exact same way. At the same time, significant challenges stem from our reliance on using an input, hours, to quantify an outcome, like productivity.

Our reliance on hours often serves to punish the most productive employees and reward the least. Too often those who get their work done faster and more effectively are only rewarded with more work, in what's commonly called *performance punishment*.[1] Poor performers, meanwhile, often experience the opposite effect, whereby being slower at completing a task requires them to log more hours, for which they are praised as being more dedicated to their work—and potentially earn more in the form of overtime pay—even if they're accomplishing as much as, or less than, their colleagues.

Nowadays, not only are hours a thoroughly insufficient metric for measuring productivity in most parts of the economy, but even output doesn't cut the mustard. Output quantifies the amount of something produced by a person, a machine, or an industry, but as many workers know, you can produce a lot of memos and reports without actually delivering results. An organization with many busy workers putting in long hours doing unnecessary tasks does not produce better outcomes than one whose staff are dedicating significantly fewer hours while remaining laser-focused on the stuff that really matters. That's why, for many organizations, we need to take our measures of performance a step further and realign our focus toward real business outcomes. Over time, as AI enables us to automate more tasks, this shift from efficiency to effectiveness will become even more pronounced, with robots managing many of the output components of today's jobs, leaving humans to focus more on driving outcomes.

Over the last century, the line between hours and true productivity has only gotten blurrier, yet our dependence on this universal measuring stick only became more entrenched.

The result is often an unhealthy relationship with work, and one that pushes us toward a less effective utilization of what is otherwise our most precious resource. If you've ever witnessed a colleague, client, or friend intentionally waste company time, take longer than necessary to complete a task to increase billings or reduce future expectations, or delay starting tasks because it was too close to the end of the day—or week, or month, or year—you know exactly what we're talking about.

Fans of the hit sitcom *Seinfeld* might recall an episode that aptly demonstrates the folly of our emphasis on hours over outcomes.[2] In it George accidentally locks his keys inside his car in the staff parking lot, forcing him to leave it there for several days. Before he hires a locksmith, he notices that his superiors have begun complimenting his job performance. That's when George realizes that his manager, an early riser, sees his car in the staff parking lot each morning and assumes George is already at his desk. The CEO, meanwhile, who typically logs more hours at night, also spots George's car in the lot on his way home each evening and starts to believe that George is burning the midnight oil. As his bosses consider promoting him, he's actually away on an unapproved vacation, prompting Jerry to observe, "Locking your keys in your car is the best career move you've ever made."

Despite all that's changed since that episode of *Seinfeld* aired in January 1996—particularly in the realms of data science, employee metrics, and workplace culture—our emphasis on hours has remained. According to Deloitte's "2024 Global Human Capital Trends" report, only 17 percent of organizations are "very or extremely effective" at measuring the value created by workers beyond tracking their activities or inputs.[3] The rest are presumably still evaluating employee effectiveness using superficial attributes—like responding to emails on time—rather than the value they drive. According to software giant Atlassian's 2024 "State of Teams" report, 65 percent of knowledge workers believe it's more important to quickly respond to messages than to make progress on key priorities.[4] In other words, a century of emphasizing time and visibility has trained employees to put more effort into looking busy than getting things done. Perhaps that is why the average desk worker spends 41 percent of their time on discretionary activities that do not add value to the business, according to research published by Harvard in 2018—and confirmed by Slack's Workforce Index, which came to an identical conclusion in 2024.[5] Asana's 2025 Anatomy of Work Index, meanwhile, found that knowledge workers spend roughly 60 percent of their time on "busy work," (what the researchers call "work about work") like attending meetings, chasing updates, and conducting check-ins. Globally, the study found the average-knowledge worker spends 103 hours in unnecessary meetings, 209 on duplicative work, and 352 just talking about work each year. As a result of these unnecessary and time-consuming tasks, 88 percent say they're falling behind on time-sensitive projects and major initiatives.[6]

These time-consuming, less-than-vital tasks are what author Cal Newport labels "pseudo work." In a blog post published in June of 2025 the *Deep Work* author says many knowledge workers are led to believe their job requirements are designed to fit precisely into the allotted 40 hours per week, in what he labels the "workload fairy tale." Newport suggests the four-day workweek shatters that myth. "The key work—the efforts that really matter—turned out to require less than forty hours a week of effort, so even with a reduced schedule, the participants could still fit it all in," he wrote. "Contrary to the workload fairy tale, much of our weekly work might be, from a strict value production perspective, optional."[7]

All of this "pseudo work" or "work about work" piled on top of actual job responsibilities also comes at a time when workers are expected to remain on-call during the nonworking hours that remain. According to Microsoft's 2025 Work Trends Index, the average worker receives 153 Teams messages per day, with about 58 arriving after hours. In 2025, chats sent outside the nine-to-five window increased 15 percent, causing nearly a third of workers to open their inboxes after 10 p.m. Meetings, similarly, are bleeding into off-hours, with those scheduled for after 8 p.m. up 16 percent in 2025. Nearly 20 percent of workers also check their email before noon on weekends, and 5 percent spend time emailing after 6 p.m. on Sundays. Microsoft concludes the growing incursion of work activities into nonworking hours has resulted in "the infinite workday," and one in three workers say it's become impossible to keep up with those heightened expectations.[8]

While many had hoped the switch to a more remote workforce after the pandemic would initiate a transition to measuring productivity according to real business outcomes instead of hours and activities, the data suggests the opposite. According to a 2024 survey of fifteen hundred American workers by BambooHR, 88 percent of remote workers take actions to prove they're online and at their desks, compared with 79 percent of in-person staff.[9] The survey found that nearly two-thirds of remote workers say they keep their messaging apps perpetually open—even on mobile devices while they're away from their desks—to signal to their teams that they're available and online, in what has been dubbed the *green status effect*. Whether they're working diligently at their desks or relaxing on the beach, as long as their workplace apps signal their online status, the workers believe they'll be credited for their dedication.

The pressure to play the role of a busy worker isn't limited to those who work remotely, either. The same BambooHR survey found that 42 percent of hybrid workers return to the office just for visibility, while 37 percent of in-person staff admit to walking around the workplace just to be seen by their colleagues and superiors.

Ironically, the pressure to look busy at work often gets in the way of actually getting work done.

All of this performative busyness, as it's been dubbed, comes at a staggering cost. According to the Atlassian study, teams are busier than ever but are accomplishing less, because "knowledge workers spend so much time planning and talking about work that it prevents them from actually doing work that matters." The study estimates that *Fortune* 500 companies lose 25 billion hours to ineffective collaboration each year, and 93 percent of executives agreed that their teams could deliver similar outcomes in *half the time* if they were to collaborate more effectively. According to Slack's Workforce Index, which analyzed the habits of more than ten thousand desk workers around the world, those who feel obligated to work after hours are 20 percent *less* productive.

While measuring impact in hours causes business leaders to lose some of the potential value their staff could provide, the effects can be far more damaging to the staff members themselves. Performative busyness can be exhausting, especially when coupled with real work demands. The Slack Workforce Index study discovered that the same employees who feel obligated to work after hours are roughly twice as likely to struggle with work-related stress, have lower job satisfaction, and are at double the risk of suffering burnout. "Being inauthentic is really tiring for people, and so the more time that somebody is in this inauthentic mode, it's not a good internal feeling for them personally, but it also takes more energy," explains John Trougakos, a professor of organizational behavior and HR management at the University of Toronto and an associate consultant at Joe's firm, Work Time Revolution. "So then when we need to do things that are actually important, we've wasted our energy doing things that are completely unimportant."[10] Not only is doing fake work exhausting and unnecessary, but it can also contribute to burnout both by pulling us away from work that will need to be made up for later and by taking away our feeling of autonomy. "When people feel that their autonomy is diminished, that's actually quite stressful," John explains. "It's much harder to do something because you feel like you must do it."

Of course, in life and in work, people will always have to do things they don't want to do—there's no getting around that. However, the research suggests that the more stuff people are forced to do against their will or without feeling as if it's important or necessary, the worse they perform and the more likely they are to burn out. "When you pile on a bunch of stuff that employees feel the organization isn't really getting any benefit from, then that is especially taxing and especially leads to burnout, because they will struggle more to find motivation," John explains. "When we're intrinsically motivated to do something, it's a lot easier."

In a knowledge economy, the correlation between hours and outcomes is far weaker than the correlation between employee well-being and outcomes, and a quick scan of the global economy starkly demonstrates this relationship. Many of the world's most economically competitive—and happiest—nations work the *fewest* hours, while some of the poorest work the longest.

In the European Union, for example, the average number of hours worked per year is 1,571, taking into account parental leave, vacation allowance, part-time work, and overtime, according to a study by the Organisation for Economic Co-operation and Development (OECD).[11] Within the bloc, however, some nations work 25 percent fewer hours than others, despite enjoying stronger-than-average economic output. At the lower end of the work hours spectrum, the Swiss work an average of 1,529 hours per year, the Swedes work 1,440, while the Danes and Germans tie for the EU's shortest work schedule, at 1,347 per year—about 26 hours a week. Those countries are also standouts for having the highest gross domestic product (GDP) per capita, the most productive workers, and—according to the annual World Happiness Report—the happiest citizenry.[12] On the opposite end of the spectrum, Poles work 1,815 hours a year, Maltese work 1,876, and Greeks work 1,886 while maintaining some of the lowest GDP per capita rates in the European Union. Worldwide, the record for most hours worked per year out of any country included in the research goes to Mexico, with an annual 2,226, or about 43 hours per week. As of this writing, there is an ongoing legislative effort to reduce Mexico's legally allowable working hours from a maximum of 48 hours per week over six days to a 40-hour standard.[13] "We are convinced that giving workers eight extra hours of free time each week will contribute to national development," said President Claudia Sheinbaum in a speech on Mexican Labor Day, May 1, 2025.[14]

The OECD data was so striking when it was published in 2022 that it had a significant role in giving our friend and Nobel Prize–winning economist Sir Christopher confidence in the inevitability of the four-day workweek. "If you look at Greece, Denmark and the Netherlands," he tells us, "they're very similar sized countries, so why should the Greeks work on average, about thirty-six, thirty-seven hours [each week] and the Danish and Dutch twenty-nine hours? It's likely because they are more productive, so they have higher incomes, so they can work fewer hours."[15]

While you might assume that wealthier and more productive countries got that way by putting in more work, Sir Christopher says their success has more to do with their ability to maximize the hours they're on the clock. Being more economical with their time enables a more relaxed approach to work—one that includes more vacation time, less overtime, more generous leave policies, and greater workplace flexibility—because they're wealthy enough to afford it. "We've got a good-enough income to have a good standard of life, and therefore can pursue the other things that give us life satisfaction," he says. That is perhaps why, as the high-output economies of Northern Europe are mandating some of the world's most generous policies for things like vacation days and parental leave, countries like Greece are allowing employers to extend the workweek to a sixth day.

———————

There is one significant outlier in the study: the United States, whose 1,800-hour annual work schedule and top economic status buck the global trend.

That, Sir Christopher says, has a lot to do with American workers' unique labor market institutions, such as weak unions, fewer legal requirements pertaining to time off, a low minimum wage, and other factors that have led to one of the highest rates of income inequality in the world.[16] The United States is, after all, the only developed nation that doesn't guarantee maternity leave. "It's got nothing to do with technology," he says. Everywhere else, higher national wealth and individual economic prosperity resulted in more time off work. In fact, while the United States has the highest GDP per capita among the G20, second place goes to the Germans, who work 35 percent less, or more than 450 fewer hours per year. While American workers clock an average of about 35 hours a week—including vacation time, sick leave, parental leave, part-time hours, and overtime hours—those in Germany average around 26.

We are not suggesting that these nations are wealthier because their citizens work fewer hours; we are merely demonstrating how little correlation there is between working hours and economic output. We also acknowledge that we are primarily citing examples from large, wealthier, more Westernized nations, but that is for good reason. First, doing so allows us to compare similar economic and cultural conditions. Second, when it comes to reducing working hours, many non-Westernized work cultures are starting from a different baseline, but even they are seeing declines. In Singapore, for example, a recent study found that average weekly working hours have dropped from 46.6 in 2010, to 41.6 in 2024.[17] A law introduced in Chile in January 2023 codified the 40-hour week, ending a long-standing 45-hour standard.[18] The year prior, Chileans averaged 1,966 hours per year, or 80 more hours per year than Greece, the most overworked EU nation, according to the OECD. A similar law in Colombia will see maximum working hours, including overtime, drop from 48 per week in 2021 to 42 by July 2026.[19] In 2018, South Korea imposed a law that limited working hours to 52 per week, including 12 hours of mandatory paid overtime, down from the previous limit of 68.[20] By 2022, the OECD found that the Korean work year was just over 1,900 hours long, longer than any nation in the EU but an improvement nonetheless.

The trend may even be catching on in China, a country infamous for its brutal 996 work culture, wherein many—especially those in the tech sector—are expected to work between 9 a.m. and 9 p.m. six days a week, totaling 72 hours.[21] In early 2025, the publicly traded Chinese e-commerce giant Zibuyu switched to a 4.5-day workweek without any change to employee compensation.[22] "Since everyone has created value together, they should enjoy the rewards," CEO Chen Caixiong told his staff in Mandarin during a companywide meeting at the start of the year. "The 4.5-day work week is the best reward for the hard work of employees." During the announcement, Caixiong, whose workforce averages twenty-eight years of age, suggested that the shorter workweek was a benefit that would be most enjoyed by the company's youngest workers.

Though the 4-day workweek may be more feasible in places where work is already limited to 40 hours, there has been a global push to reduce working hours across the globe in recent years for many of the same reasons. According to the Singapore government's Ministry of Manpower, global average weekly working hours have been trending downward for at least a decade, falling from 46 in 2014 to 43 in 2024.[23]

Paradoxical as it may sound, the countries that take the most breaks ultimately accomplish the most in the long run, and research has found the same to be true at the organizational and individual levels.[24]

Fans of professional basketball are probably familiar with a controversial policy known around the National Basketball Association (NBA) as *load management*. These days, NBA superstars are enjoying longer careers because they're being given more time off. Playing sports at an elite level takes a significant physical toll, and many professional athletes now prescribe to a regimen that includes sufficient rest and recovery to reduce the likelihood of injury. Of course, the league and many of its fans aren't happy to see star players sitting on the sidelines during inconsequential regular-season games, but you don't hear them complaining as much about seeing an entire generation of future hall-of-famers (like LeBron James, Stephen Curry, Kevin Durant, Chris Paul, James Harden, etc.) not just remaining in the league but contributing at a high level late into their careers.

There's a similar challenge when it comes to rallying support for rest and recovery in a workforce that still equates hours with productivity. "There's a body of evidence that's twenty-five years old now, and it's pretty definitive, that getting time away from work is actually really important to being productive at work," explains John Trougakos, professor at University of Toronto Scarborough. Part of this research, which John has contributed to directly, is the well-documented diminishing rate of return on work time.[25] According to the data, people take some time to warm up to a task, and then they reach peak performance levels before an inevitable decrease. As time wears on, they not only become less effective but are also more likely to make a critical error.

According to a 2025 study published in the journal *Occupational and Environmental Medicine*, working more than fifty-two hours a week causes physical changes in areas of the brain associated with emotional regulation and executive function.[26] "Our findings highlight the need to prioritize mental health, regular rest periods, and work-life balance to preserve cognitive and emotional health," Wanhyung Lee, one of the study's coauthors told Jared in an email interview for a story that published in the *Globe and Mail*.[27] Lee also cautioned that the risks are far more pronounced in a digital world, where work is much less confined to specific hours.

The research also reinforces what we already know about mental energy and performance. "As people get tired, the more they push themselves through, the more errors they make," John says, adding that people can sustain higher levels of peak productivity when they're intrinsically motivated. "When you're really, really motivated to do something for the inherent enjoyment of the task or the meaning the task has for you, you can push yourself further and are able to do it more effectively for longer, because it's not really draining you in the same way."

John's research also finds a direct correlation between the length and quality of time away from work and the ability to perform at peak levels. In a 2023 study, he and his colleagues measured fluctuations in emotional exhaustion throughout the workday.[28] They found that there are day-to-day variances, but emotional exhaustion tends to subscribe to certain predictable patterns over the long run. "What we find is that when people go to work, they start off at a certain level of emotional exhaustion, and when you work, emotional exhaustion tends to increase across the workday," he says. "One of the primary drivers that determines where people are going to start on the emotional exhaustion scale each day is their psychological detachment from work the previous day." In other words, John and his colleagues found that both the frequency and the quality of breaks has a direct and measurable impact on our ability to perform at work. "The more effective they are at taking those opportunities to get away from work, the less fatigued they are, the more productive they are, and the better they perform."

Unfortunately, the current workplace culture around breaks is anything but healthy. Instead of encouraging rest, we stigmatize it, with workplace hero culture celebrating those who stay up late, eat at their desks, work through the weekend, and skip vacations. According to a 2024 global survey of 11,500 workers by Expedia, 62 percent don't feel like they have enough time off for breaks.[29] The study also found that Americans take the least time off, with the average worker allotted just eleven days a year, and half using less than their full time-off allotment. According to a survey by Pew Research, half don't avail themselves of their full vacation entitlement out of fear of falling behind at work, and 43 percent say they feel bad for asking their coworkers to pick up the slack, including almost half of female respondents.[30] In a 2025 study published in the journal *Organizational Behavior and Human Decision Processes*, managers acknowledged workers were more energized and productive after detaching from work. However, they also admitted to penalizing staff who do so regularly, viewing them as less committed and less worthy of promotion in what the researchers labelled the "detachment paradox."[31]

Though many still consider working fewer hours and taking more frequent breaks as a negative contributor to productivity, the research suggests the opposite. Long hours instead create a double-negative compounding effect on employee health—the direct toll of increased mental and physical strain, and the indirect shrinking of opportunities for mental or physical rest and recovery. The diminishing rate of return on hourly productivity from working excessive hours means that any short-term benefits are unsustainable and ultimately eaten up in the long run by the costs of employee burnout, turnover, and disengagement. According to a 2025 study published in the *American Journal of Preventive Medicine*, employee burnout costs American businesses between $4,000 and $21,000 per employee per year in the form of higher health-care coverage and absenteeism.[32] That's about $5 million annually for a company of a thousand. Like elite athletes, giving ourselves time to rest and recover has a long-term positive effect on physical energy and mental bandwidth, allowing us to perform at our highest levels, rather than for the most hours.

To combat some of these effects, employers have sought to implement various wellness programs, though they often prove ineffective. A recent study from Oxford University found that only one in ninety corporate wellness initiatives has any demonstratively positive impact on employee well-being.[33] It's a staggering statistic, but not all that surprising, given that burnout rates are increasing and that many corporate wellness programs don't address root causes like unsustainable workloads, unreasonable expectations, and unclear boundaries. (Ironically, the only one of those 90 that proved effective was volunteering, something the four-day workweek enables, as demonstrated by trial participants.)

Like so many other (often well-intentioned) corporate policies, offering access to yoga classes, meditation apps, and cold plunge clubs is often like putting a Band-Aid on a deep wound. Though they might give the organization permission to check the mental well-being box and move on, those challenges need a more systemic fix, and the four-day workweek is proving itself a more effective and lasting solution. According to think tank Infinite Potential's study, workplace burnout affected 42 percent of employees working a standard forty-hour workweek in 2024, up from 38 percent in 2023.[34] The research, which sampled data from many of Joe's clients, found that burnout rates among employees at organizations operating on a thirty-two-hour weekly schedule were just 9 percent.

Organizations are projected to spend $94.6 billion globally on corporate wellness solutions by 2026, even though the results thus far have been mixed at best.[35] A four-day workweek program, meanwhile, typically comes at little or no cost and has been proven widely effective in improving employee mental health and well-being.

———————

Thirty years after George locked his keys in the car, workers are still more likely to be praised and promoted for being seen at the office early in the morning and late into the evening than for actually getting work done effectively.

The four-day workweek, at its core, is an attempt to cut down on wasted time, not in the interest of more intensive work but in the interest of more leisure time—which, in a knowledge economy, can improve overall outcomes. That sentiment is well founded in John's research, which demonstrates how working fewer hours can net greater outcomes than overworking. What's missing is a willingness to measure effectiveness based on outcomes—the quality of hours, not the quantity.

As described earlier, we have long moved away from an industrial economy, yet many of our basic work structures and norms have been adopted from it. Chief among them is our approach to measuring productivity as output over number of hours. Now that we've transitioned to a knowledge economy—an economy that is designed to leverage the power of the human brain—we need a new way of working, a way that promotes healthier, more productive brains. A kind of mental-load management for the all-star employee.

As John's research found, the most effective way to maximize the collective brainpower of the workforce is by promoting a healthy balance of rest and recovery. If you measure productivity in hours, the four-day workweek represents a massive loss. If you measure productivity in outcomes, it's a massive gain.

———————

Evolving to a model where work is measured not in hours but in outcomes requires a completely different approach to the very concept of productivity.

In an ideal world, everyone would spend some time working closely with their manager or employer to clearly define exactly what's expected of them each day, week, month, quarter, or year. Through that process, both the worker and the employer arrive at a mutual understanding of what constitutes strong performance, adequate performance, and poor performance in terms that do not include a measurement of time. Maybe it's a sales quota, maybe it's customer service response time, maybe it's an opening statement for an upcoming trial. Whatever that thing is that has to get done, in this ideal world both the worker and their manager know what success looks like and how it will be measured objectively, regardless of how long it takes.

That approach ultimately leaves individual workers free to do the thing they're responsible for doing on whatever timeline best suits their needs (not unlike farmers or cottage industry workers of the preindustrial era). If a worker needs a whole day to complete that task, they will dedicate the whole day to doing so. If, however, they adopt new ways of getting the thing done to that mutually agreed-on standard—as Jared did in his freelance career—whatever time is left over becomes theirs to enjoy. In this ideal world, compensation wouldn't necessarily be tied to seniority, past work experience, or where an individual went to school but would reflect the precise value they bring to the organization. If they can do more in the same or less time and thus deliver more value, they are compensated accordingly.

Though it may seem like a pipe dream, this vision could soon become a reality, thanks to AI and the broader data revolution that's already underway. For better or worse, employers are quickly gaining new ways of measuring business performance to a degree that would have seemed like science fiction just a few years ago. Taking another example from Jared's world, the Hemingway app uses AI to measure not just the quality of any writing entered by users but the school grade reading level while highlighting opportunities for improvement. There are similar tools popping up all over the place, with new technologies measuring and quantifying performance in more granular ways that don't default to hours.

When these tools are coupled with our traditional reliance on hours as a measurement of productivity, however, there is a real danger that they could be used to squeeze every drop of energy and efficiency out of workers, without them sharing in the rewards. In that more pessimistic view, performance metrics are primarily used to surveil employees, increase output expectations, and punish lower performers. In a healthier work environment, however, they can be used to set a universal bar that, once cleared, leaves workers free to either work harder for bonus compensation or take the remainder of the allotted time off from work. Though it's still early days, many organizations are adopting this results-only work environment style of work, where teams are given tasks and deadlines, clear objectives and expectations, and the freedom to craft their own schedules in a way that best suits their needs.

The question that remains is whether we'll utilize these new tools to evolve beyond measuring outcomes based on hours and activities or use them to impose higher standards and requirements on workers. As technologies like AI and automation take over some of the more repetitive and robotic tasks, workers will be valued for their most human skills. After all, AI can transcribe and summarize Jared's interview notes, but it will be a long time before it can conduct those interviews. To borrow another example shared earlier, some writers and journalists fear that AI will come to replace their jobs; Jared believes its effects will probably be more like that of the calculator on the accounting profession, freeing him from more menial tasks to deliver higher-value work.

AI tools will enable humans to do many of their work tasks infinitely faster and more efficiently or outsource them to AI entirely, forcing a re-evaluation of our traditional understanding of "productivity." In that future getting a little extra effort—a few extra hours or a couple extra drops of efficiency—out of workers is much less important than optimizing their ability to do those things that AI can't.

As we enter a world of work that once again values our most human traits, the most effective employees will be those who can maximize their focus, energy, and creativity. That, according to the research, means frequent breaks, adequate recovery time, and a strong work-life balance, each of which is better accomplished on a four-day schedule. The extra day off also acts as a strong motivator for teams to remain accountable to each other and themselves. If we reward teams for delivering efficiency gains and process improvements by sharing the spoils of their efforts with them in the form of extra time for themselves, we will increase their motivation to adopt new ways of working, to shift mindsets, and to better engage with broader organizational transformation efforts. Some of today's workplace challenges, such as ineffective collaboration, excessive administration, digital distraction, and a disregard for de-prioritization, are deeply embedded. Piloting a shorter workweek can act as an organizational call to arms for a war on busywork, which threatens both well-being and productivity.

6 The Kids Are All Right

After enjoying a shorter schedule for six months during the trial period, employees of the forty-one participating organizations in the North American pilot program were asked to put a dollar value on their new working schedule.

One-third said they would demand a salary increase of between 26 percent and 50 percent to switch back to a five-day schedule, 12 percent said they would demand more than 50 percent more, and 14 percent said no amount of money would persuade them to return to a five-day rotation.[1] "It would definitely be difficult to persuade me to return to a five-day workweek after experiencing the benefits and flexibility a four-day workweek offers," says Anisah Hooda-Tarbhai, a twenty-six-year-old program associate for Grand Challenges Canada, which participated in the North American pilot program. "It's hard to quantify how much the four-day workweek has given me in terms of the mental health and physical health benefits."[2]

Anisah joined the Canadian arm of the global nonprofit in 2019 and watched as it gradually reduced its schedule requirements. First the company offered summer Fridays, then flexible Fridays, and, finally, a four-day workweek with Fridays off. While she says the reduced schedule wasn't why she joined the company, this benefit—coupled with her passion for the organization's core mission—has made it nearly impossible to leave.

Like many second-generation immigrants, Anisah grew up in a household that had to make difficult sacrifices in pursuit of economic stability for the children. Her parents, both East African immigrants who co-owned a signage and graphic design business, often worked around the clock, a practice that Anisah says informed her perspective on work-life balance. "They really gave it everything," she says. "I understand the sacrifices that they made to get us where we are today, but I also saw the toll that it took on their physical health, mental health, family life, etc. And I always kind of wanted something different for myself, something that allowed me to spend a bit more time with my family while still being able to meet my needs."

These days, Anisah says her Fridays typically begin with a workout and include an afternoon walk when weather permits. "I tend to do a lot of my general admin work—appointments, grocery shopping, cleaning from everything that's accumulated over the week," she says. "I kind of split everything that I would usually do over the weekend, like rushing to squeeze in appointments, rushing to do groceries, rushing to clean the house—and put it onto the Friday, so I'm able to actually enjoy my weekend."

Despite taking more time for herself, Anisah says the reduced schedule has also had a positive impact on the quality of her work. She explains that her role, which includes coordinating with organizations and individuals operating in conflict zones and resource-constrained settings around the world, can be overwhelming at times. The extra day off allows her to adequately recover from what can be an emotionally draining job.

She also says her organization has evolved to embrace the four-day schedule by dramatically cutting meeting frequency, duration, and participant numbers; incorporating new technologies that can help automate and streamline tasks; and realigning priorities to focus on outcomes. "I've also learned to be more efficient, like time-blocking my calendar for focused work," she says. "Having Friday to decompress has allowed me to be more focused during those four days and get a lot more done than what I would have Friday, because you just get mentally fatigued by the end of the week; cutting out that last day really allows you to run at a higher percentage and work more efficiently." Of course, there are still weeks when Anisah's workload makes it hard to take the day off, but she says that in those crunch times, getting meaningful work done becomes much easier on Fridays, thanks to an otherwise clear schedule.

Anisah adds that the value she puts on work-life balance, the way she connects mental and physical well-being to her ability to perform in her job, and her prioritization of time over money are all common among her peers. "I think that we're a generation that's finally putting ourselves first; we want to be the best versions of ourselves, for ourselves but also for those around us. And I can't be that if I'm commuting to the office five days a week for an hour and a half each way, because I'm just not able to show up as the best version of myself," she explains. "Those nonmonetary benefits, for our generation, are taking priority over actual salary."

That is not to say that younger workers don't care about their compensation—quite the contrary, in today's world of rising costs and depleting affordability. At the same time, Anisah argues that the higher cost of living has made it harder for her generation to manage caregiving and personal responsibilities, as single-income households become less feasible. The heightened expectation on young people today—and especially women—to be both earners and caretakers is simply too much for most to manage on a five-day work schedule. "The reality is most households have two working parents," she says. "We're still able to show up at work, but we'd like the opportunity to show up for our families at home as well. And remote working opportunities and flexible arrangements such as the four-day workweek allow for the best of both worlds, where I can show up at 100 percent at work during those four days."

Anisah believes that for all these reasons, the four-day workweek is not just necessary but inevitable—if not in the short term, then in a future when those in her generation start their own families and occupy more leadership positions. "As Gen Z enters into those phases of life, they'll empathize with individuals in those situations and want to create an environment in which everyone feels valued and welcomed at work," she says. "In order to retain employees and to really allow them to feel valued, all of those things will really come together in terms of advocating for the four-day workweek, for flexible working arrangements, for mental and physical health being prioritized at the workplace, and I think that will all be amplified as Gen Z works their way up the corporate ladder."

———————

Most Nobel Prize–winning economic research papers are dense and difficult for your average noneconomist to decipher. The paper that won our friend Sir Christopher and his co-researchers the coveted award in 2010, he admits, is fairly straightforward.[3]

Sir Christopher explains that he and his colleagues used mathematical formulas to show that *search theory*—which suggests businesses will shape their products and services in response to the attributes that customers actively search for—also applies to the labor market. Just as private businesses in a free market respond to consumer demands, so too will employers offer work perks and career opportunities sought by workers. Or, as he puts it, "A market that is free of excess regulation and a central command economy will sooner or later respond to what the workers want in the way that they respond to what the consumers want in a marketing framework."

This principle, he tells us, is what has given rise in recent years to diversity and inclusion initiatives, more-sustainable business practices, and workplace flexibility—not the goodness of employers' hearts but the reality that offering those attributes improves their ability to attract and retain young talent. "If you give workers what they want in the market, then they're going to be more productive when they come to work with you," adds Sir Christopher. "They're going to be happier at work, they're going to have incentives to work harder, they have incentives to collaborate with you—rather than try and cheat you or laze about when there isn't direct supervision—and that's the whole idea."

Part of what led Sir Christopher to connect that research to the four-day workweek—in addition to the launch of ChatGPT and the OECD data on average working hours by nation, as explored in previous chapters—was a study by the American Psychological Association.[4] It found that one-third of workers believe a four-day workweek is an effective way for employers to support their staff's well-being at work. The study demonstrated how an employee perk that seemed unimaginable just years prior was now on employees' radar, and Sir Christopher's research suggests that once employees identify and demand such perks, employers are likely to respond.

In fact, the data suggests that this employer response has since played out as expected. Between June 2023 and June 2024, searches for jobs with reduced-hour workweek models increased by 68 percent on Flexa, a job platform dedicated to flexible work. During that time, interest in a four-day workweek doubled, interest in a four-and-a-half-day workweek tripled, and searches for jobs that offered a nine-day fortnight (one less day every two weeks) quadrupled. In a 2025 survey of UK-based workers conducted by Owl Labs, 83 percent predicted the four-day workweek will be more common than the current five-day standard by 2030, including 91 percent of Gen Z respondents.[5]

Given the lingering mental health crisis that began during the pandemic and the rising costs of managing those challenges in the form of health care, absenteeism, worker engagement, and turnover, Sir Christopher believed that employers would inevitably pursue the solutions that workers identified as most effective.

According to his research, however, employers are unlikely to offer an employee benefit that workers don't believe the company can realistically attain. As Sir Christopher considered which attributes might become the subject of the next generation of employees' searches, the four-day workweek stood out to him as the most likely contender. "It's like diversity, or environmentally friendly companies, or flexibility; all these things will eventually get implemented. We're going to see them happening in the market because there is demand," he says. "So, the quicker they prepare for the four-day workweek, the better off companies will be."

————————————————

In the summer of 2024, Squarespace's chief marketing officer, Kinjil Mathur, attracted criticism when she told Gen Z job seekers that they, like her, should be "willing to do anything" to land their first job.

"I was willing to work for free, I was willing to work any hours they needed—even on evenings and weekends," Kinjil told *Fortune*. "You really have to just be willing to do anything, any hours, any pay, any type of job." The online backlash to Kinjil's statement was immediate and brutal, forcing her to walk those comments back. "I shared my own college internship experiences, and my words were misrepresented as career advice for a whole generation," Kinjil later said in a statement.[6]

The episode demonstrates a growing clash of values between the various generations in today's workplace. While some still take pride in sacrificing their well-being to demonstrate their commitment, others—primarily younger workers—see things differently. "I think they have more of an attitude of work-to-live as opposed to live-to-work that many of us grew up with," said Ravin Jesuthasan, the global leader for transformation services at the consulting giant Mercer, on stage in Davos in 2024.[7] "This is particularly true in the West. They have seen the legacy of all these broken promises. In the old days and in many parts of the West, they would promise you if you worked for 30 years, you'd have this defined benefit pension, you'd have retiree medical care, etc. None of that exists today."

One of the many points of differentiation between today's young people and older workers is their perception of stress. Historically, Western workplace cultures equated stress with importance. If you were stressed, it often meant your job was more demanding and thus more important, encouraging some to complain about stress as a way to subtly communicate their value. Rather than seeing *stress bragging*—or talking about being overworked with a sense of pride—as a badge of honor, however, young people are more likely to interpret it as indicative of poor time management at best and an unhealthy relationship with work at worst. According to a 2024 study by researchers at the University of Georgia, those who brag the most about being stressed are now perceived more negatively by their peers.[8] In fact, the research suggests those who stress brag are perceived as *less* capable, not more. After generations of equating time with effectiveness and busyness with importance, Gen Z has come to view the value of their time through a different lens.

It's not just that Gen Z grew up in an era when many of the traditional promises of work and loyalty had long since been broken, and when individual time commitments had been largely divorced from actual results. Those born in the late 1990s through the early 2010s have also already lived through a once-in-a-century economic crisis, endured a once-in-a-century pandemic, and are regularly bombarded by what were formerly considered once-in-a-century extreme weather events. This generation, which is just entering the workforce, spent their childhoods hearing their parents panic over financial challenges during the 2008 economic crisis, had their brains shaped by an unregulated social media machine that has proven detrimental to their mental health, lost some of their formative years to pandemic restrictions and lockdowns, and continues to face a barrage of new challenges almost daily.

More so than any generation before them, this group of young people has developed an appreciation for proper time management, mental health, and well-being. Their well-documented emphasis on meaning and joy has come to replace past generations' keeping-up-with-the-Joneses competitive pursuit of material wealth. People say that money can't buy happiness, but the most anxious and depressed generation in modern history has internalized that sentiment.

Countless studies show that when it comes to their priorities in life—and at work—Gen Zers seek a greater balance between economic and emotional stability, prizing quality time over financial excess. According to a 2023 survey by Intuit, three-quarters of Gen Zers say they would rather have a better quality of life than more money in the bank, and 66 percent say they are only interested in earning money as a way to support their personal interests.[9] Part of the motivation, the study suggests, is that social comparison has evolved from homes, cars, and other material markers of wealth to social media posts. In fact, 33 percent of Gen Z members said they compare themselves to people they see on social media, versus 14 percent of the general population, and 70 percent say they feel as if they're falling behind those they see online, compared with 50 percent of others. In Deloitte's 2024 survey of millennials and Gen Zers, the respondents ranked work-life balance as their top priority when choosing an employer, followed by flexible hours and reduced workweeks—all of which outranked salary.[10]

In short, Anisah's is the perfect generation to champion a shorter workweek. Not only does the reduced schedule offer more leisure time, which this generation prizes over compensation, but it has also been proven to reduce stress, anxiety, burnout, and depression. Furthermore, the four-day workweek represents an opportunity to address some of their greatest collective challenges, like improving family and community ties in the digital age, improving gender equity, and addressing climate change (more on that in the next chapter). Finally, the four-day workweek offers this generation more time to engage in causes that are meaningful to them, a primary motivator for younger workers, according to research.

———

Gen Z is also the most enthusiastic generation about the concept of a four-day workweek and the most convinced of not just its feasibility but also its inevitability.

In a 2024 survey of Gen Z students and professionals in the United States aged eighteen to twenty-seven, 80 percent said the four-day week should be standard, up from 76 percent the previous year.[11] The same study also found that most young people were already utilizing new AI technologies to get more done in less time, with 72 percent saying they felt comfortable using generative AI regularly. In fact, 72 percent of Gen Z AI users said they save between one and ten hours of schoolwork per week by leveraging the technology, and 14 percent have reduced their work time by more than 10 hours.

Young people are so keen on a shorter workweek that they're even willing to forgo other traditional workplace perks. In a 2023 survey by Bankrate, 92 percent of Gen Z and millennial respondents said they would sacrifice other common benefits in exchange for a four-day workweek, compared with 89 percent of Gen Xers and 80 percent of baby boomers.[12] The most common workplace perks and norms that respondents of all generations would sacrifice for one less workday is the eight-hour day, with 54 percent saying they would work longer hours during the remaining four days. The second-most-popular trade-off was changing industries, jobs, or companies, with 37 percent saying they would leave their current role for a shorter schedule. According to a 2023 survey of twelve thousand workers in the United Kingdom by Hays, 62 percent would prefer to work a four-day workweek in the office rather than a traditional five-day hybrid schedule.[13] In its 2025 annual review, global HR firm Randstad, which has been asking thousands of workers around the world about work preferences since 2004, found that they ranked work-life balance ahead of pay for the first time.[14] In the company's global survey of twenty-six thousand workers, 83 percent put it at the very top of their priority list, and this preference was even stronger among Gen Z workers.

For Anisah's colleague Raheeb Rahman, the four-day workweek also offers young people a smoother transition from academia to the workforce.

The twenty-two-year-old accounting and finance student at the Ted Rogers School of Management at Toronto Metropolitan University says he got positive responses from many of the internships he applied to but that Grand Challenges Canada stood out for its mission and values. "Being a not-for-profit organization, that was also unique—not a lot of students get that opportunity," he says. "The other thing that stood out for me about Grand Challenges Canada during the application process was the four-day workweek."[15] Despite being unfamiliar with Parkinson's law—that "work expands so as to fill the time available for its completion"—Raheeb appears to have come up with the theory on his own, from his experience with his schoolwork. "In university, when you're completing projects—even with a shorter deadline—as long as it's a reasonable deadline, we are still able to complete our projects and assignments on time," he says. "Let's say I have a project that's four months long—if I start a month late, I'm still able to complete that same project within three months."

Raheeb also felt that the shorter workweek could help ease his transition into the workforce, given that his current academic schedule is typically condensed into four days. "It's up to us to manage our time and manage our well-being, implementing our own eating, sleeping, and exercise habits," he says. "We're now at an age where we are able to kind of create the lifestyle that we really want." For Raheeb, that lifestyle involves prayer, volunteering, biking, and walking, though he admits not all university students have the same priorities. At the same time, he acknowledges that college is often considered the best years of a person's life because this period is their first—and perhaps only—opportunity to prioritize their time in any way they want as long as they meet their academic responsibilities.

Raheeb, like many young people, was just getting used to the autonomy and personal responsibility afforded to postsecondary students when it came time to start looking for an internship and, later, his first full-time job. Like many of his peers, Raheeb wasn't so keen to let go of that autonomy upon entering the workforce, and for this reason, the four-day workweek was particularly appealing. As he makes the transition from student to intern to employee, Raheeb says he's thinking about freedom and flexibility as much as, or more than, compensation. "At the end of the day, if there's a company that respects our well-being in different ways with the perks or flexibility that they provide, I think that's something that I will prioritize, not necessarily who provides the highest salary."

As Raheeb articulates, university graduates enter the workforce having experienced a study environment built on autonomy, empowerment, and accountability for outcomes. After proving themselves capable of self-management, they are immediately plunged into a work environment that is typically built for command and control. The switch often proves jarring, limiting the potential of younger workers who are often keen to perform in their early careers but who struggle under a culture of micromanagement.

Even if other generations are slow to take up the cause, there is good reason to believe the four-day workweek is inevitable—because it will be so highly valued by a generation of future leaders.

Anisah says that her parents sometimes poke fun at her more relaxed work arrangement, but through the jokes is a certain sense of pride that they've been able to give their children a better life than the one they had. Furthermore, as they phase into retirement, Anisah says she's finally getting back some of the time her parents had to sacrifice in her childhood now that they can spend their Fridays together. "They make sarcastic comments about, like, 'Do you even work?'" she says. "But I think they're proud that I was able to work my way into a company that allows for this balance, because I think it's something that they would have wanted for themselves, and of course parents only want better for their children. I think that that comes through more so than anything."

7 The Bigger Picture of a Shorter Workweek

Did you know you could surf in New York City?

We certainly didn't, at least not until we joined a video call with Jon Leland. The then chief strategy officer and head of sustainability for Brooklyn-based crowdfunding platform Kickstarter resembled a young Bob Dylan when he joined our meeting, wearing sunglasses indoors to shield his eyes from the undraped windows of his Queens apartment. There in the background, much to our surprise, sat a sitar—an Indian guitar-like instrument with three times the strings—and a surfboard, which seemed a little out of place in the otherwise quintessential New York City setting. "JFK airport is right over there," he says, pointing outside his uncovered window, while further shielding his aviator-covered eyes from the sun with his hand.[1] "The next island over is Rockaway Beach, then you have Atlantic Beach, where you have this series of little barrier islands and peninsulas just on the ocean." If you assumed surfing in New York City would be a very seasonal activity, Jon says you'd be wrong there, too. "January is actually the best time to go," he suggests, a claim we can't refute using anything resembling firsthand knowledge.

Jon is something of a pioneer in the four-day workweek movement and is one of its public faces, having argued on its behalf at a

US Senate hearing in March 2024. Like most New Yorkers—and most people, for that matter—the longtime climate activist says he struggled with the isolation, loneliness, and sheer boredom brought by the pandemic in 2020 and 2021. The restriction on movement, however, opened the door to a certain freedom of thought, and Jon found his understimulated brain fixating on a challenge he had spent much of his adult life trying to solve. "I've always been interested in climate messaging and how difficult it is," he says. "The data is scary, the warning signs are real, and a lot of the solutions require a kind of personal sacrifice, so there's this guilt and this bleak vision of the future attached to it."

Around that time, Jon began reading about the four-day workweek and had something of an epiphany. What if the messaging around climate change wasn't scary, wasn't designed to make us feel guilty, or asked us to make personal sacrifices? What if being better stewards of the environment was additive, not reductive, a benefit rather than a sacrifice? Jon says that the four-day workweek is "an interesting lever, both because it is a more optimistic vision of the future and it's something that everyone wants, which is different from what you usually get with climate action. It also speaks to the cultural psychology of having more balance: more work-life balance, and more balance between nature and consumption."

Jon's hypothesis about the four-day workweek being a more sustainable alternative to the five-day standard was based on a 2014 study, which found that Europeans and North Americans have lower carbon footprints on weekends.[2] In fact, their emissions on Sundays were 40 percent lower than the overall daily average, and 20 percent higher on weekdays. Data from the US Energy Information Administration also shows that Americans burn 10 percent less fossil fuels on weekends than on weekdays.[3] "If we can convert a weekday into a weekend day, that's going to reduce carbon emissions for that day by 10 percent," Jon says. Transportation makes up 28 percent of US emissions, and commercial and residential buildings make up another 13 percent, according to the US Environmental Protection

Agency.[4] It therefore stands to reason that having offices, highways, and factories sit empty for one extra day would result in significant emissions reductions. "There's more miles driven on weekdays than on weekends—about 14 percent more miles," he adds, suggesting that four days of rush-hour traffic is a huge improvement from five. "Based on those two factors, that adds up to about 48 million tons of carbon reduction per year on a national scale."

Other research backs Jon's hypothesis about the four-day workweek's being an effective climate reduction strategy. A 2012 study from the University of Massachusetts, for example, found that a 10 percent reduction in work time among OECD member nations would lead to decreases in their ecological footprint, carbon footprint, and CO_2 emissions by 12.1 percent, 14.6 percent, and 4.2 percent, respectively.[5] Research from the Chalmers University of Technology in Sweden found that a decrease in work time by 1 percent reduces energy use and greenhouse gas emissions by about 0.8 percent.[6] When the coastal city of València, Spain, carried out a citywide four-day workweek trial in the spring of 2023, it measured a 58 percent reduction in nitrous oxide in the city's air.[7]

Reducing working hours doesn't only take more vehicles off the road during rush hour and reduce the electricity needs of skyscrapers and factories by a significant margin. The researchers studying Joe's four-day workweek pilots in the United States and United Kingdom ultimately found that the trial participants were adopting more-sustainable practices, and upon deeper reflection, it stands to reason. When work consumes a larger proportion of your day, you seldom have the luxury of making decisions you know are better for yourself or the environment in the long run. For example, people who feel more of a time crunch in their everyday lives are much less likely to ride their bikes to work rather than drive, and they are less likely to cook a healthy meal rather than order takeout. The rat race of corporate life encourages us to prioritize convenience, even when we know those decisions aren't in our personal or collective interest in the long term. Perhaps that is why the UK trial participants reported that the four-day workweek had made them more environmentally conscious. In fact, in both the US and UK trials, the participants told the researchers that they spent more of their time off engaging in low-emitting activities like biking and jogging and spent more time outdoors, inspiring a different relationship with the natural world. The trial participants in the United Kingdom also spent more time volunteering for environmental causes, were more conscious of household recycling practices, and were more likely to buy more eco-friendly products after they started working four days a week.

You could argue that much of the environmental benefits of switching to a four-day workweek have already been realized by the widespread switch to remote work, but those energy savings aren't universal, and research suggests they're also in decline. At the height of the pandemic, in April 2020, nearly half of the US workforce operated on a fully remote basis, according to a Gallup study, including 70 percent of those with jobs that could be done from home.[8] By 2023, only 12.7 percent of full-time American employees worked remotely, including just 27 percent of those with jobs that could be done from home.[9] According to the US Census Bureau, about 76 percent of American workers over the age of sixteen said they drove to work alone daily each year the data was collected, starting in 2006 and continuing right up to 2020.[10] That year, the bureau was unable to collect the data, but when it started up again, the figure hadn't dropped as much as you might expect. Despite the rise of remote work in 2021, that year 67.8 percent of employed Americans drove to work alone every day, and that figure has been steadily climbing ever since, as more organizations increase in-person days or enact return-to-office policies. By January 2025, roughly 29 percent of paid workdays in the United States were spent at home.[11]

The emissions associated with in-person work also means that organizations seeking to bring workers back into the office while reducing their overall footprint will find themselves choosing between their return-to-office policies and their sustainability goals. The four-day workweek can help balance the scales by allowing organizations to increase in-person collaboration without a significant increase in the emissions required to run their business.

On discovering the potential environmental impact of a four-day workweek, Jon decided to go all in on bringing the concept to America's (surfable) shores.

"I put in $60,000 of my own money to hire a team to start working on this issue," he says, explaining that the funds went toward bankrolling the first four-day workweek pilot in the United States, in 2021, which was coordinated by Joe. "That money was instrumental in getting the concept over here," he adds. After the conclusion of that first US trial in early 2022—which Jon supported in his personal capacity as a climate activist alone—he decided to bring the four-day workweek to his own workplace. "I wrote a memo to lay out the research on the issue to date and outline what a pilot would look like—the benefits and risks associated with it—and tried to make it as clear and objective as possible," he says. "I was transparent that I was working outside of my job on this issue, so I was partial, but I tried to present it as objectively as possible because I think the issue makes a case for itself."

At the time Kickstarter—which has raised nearly $9 billion to fund about 280,000 projects as of mid-2025—had recently become the technology industry's first unionized workforce.[12] "At that point, we were still in negotiations on the collective bargaining agreement, and we saw [the four-day workweek] as something we could introduce that would be helpful for strengthening that relationship between the union and our employees," he says. "There were some additional risks for us using it in that context, and we put it in the collective bargaining agreement that we had the flexibility as management to move forward or not after a trial, rather than something that is required by the contract." After the trial proved successful, Jon says the company's 150 staff were permitted to maintain a four-day schedule as long as team members continued to hit their targets and objectives. Five years later, the policy is yet to be withdrawn.

What's a day worth to you?

It probably depends on how you spend it. There are days that are irreplaceable, magical, the stuff of lasting, cherished memories and those that are immediately lost to history. Some days we want to forget, some we want to hang on to forever, and some really don't mean much one way or another. The four-day workweek is a lot of things, but at its core, it's an attempt to give everyone many more of those great days and far fewer of those inconsequential ones. According to people who already enjoy a shorter workweek, that extra time off from work can be truly life-changing, with benefits that extend from their workplaces to their homes, to their communities, and, by extension, to society at large.

Just think about what you could do with an extra day off from work each week. You could spend more time traveling *and* more quality time with loved ones at home. You could spend more time exercising *and* more time relaxing. You could sleep in later *and* tackle more of your to-do list. You could read more, volunteer more, spend more time with loved ones, engage in your community, or escape into nature.

When asked how they spend their extra day off, the UK trial participants reported taking up new hobbies that they couldn't have pursued previously or returning to old ones that had long been abandoned after not being able to fit them into their weekly schedule. A few participants also used their fifth day to undertake professional qualifications. One person described using a day off to take a grandparent on weekly outings, saying that the time together meant so much to both of them and wouldn't have been possible otherwise.

The shorter workweek offers significant benefits to individuals, as we showed in the previous chapters, and significant benefits to organizations, as we'll explore further in the pages ahead, but many advocates suggest its greatest impacts may be on society at large. The four-day workweek isn't a panacea for the world's ills, but it does offer meaningful progress toward tackling some of our greatest challenges, including gender equity, family cohesion, community participation, birth rate declines, and the fight against climate change.

While it does offer employers a strategy for improving their internal workplace culture, the four-day schedule also provides the opportunity to improve the communities in which they and their staff operate. Such community building efforts, research suggests, can help employers attract and retain better workers and even sell more products. According to a 2020 study conducted by UK consulting firm Kantar, brands with a high sense of purpose had a valuation 175 percent higher than those that didn't over the previous twelve years.[13] They also grew 86 percent over that time, compared with the 70 percent growth rate achieved by brands with a low sense of purpose. In fact, 76 percent of global market leaders have a well-defined corporate purpose. Furthermore, nearly two-thirds of millennial and Gen Z consumers said they prefer buying from brands that stand for something. A 2022 survey conducted by LinkedIn showed that 82 percent of American workers said they want to work for an organization whose culture and values align with their own.[14]

As discussed earlier, employees—especially younger employees—are taking environmental, social, and governance (ESG) efforts into consideration as they make employment decisions, and as Sir Christopher explains, those demands will inevitably force employers to respond. Salary is important, but most employees view earning potential as just one of many factors that they consider as they navigate their careers. If ESG was once mostly corporate posturing or box-checking, a new generation of workers are forcing employers to take things like meaning, mission, and values seriously. Becoming an employer of choice, especially among younger generations, requires communicating a strong sense of brand purpose.

The value of such initiatives is also proven by the recent rise of benefit corporations, or B Corps. The prestigious Certified B Corporation accreditation is awarded to for-profit organizations that meet high standards for "social and environmental performance, transparency, and accountability."[15] Thus far, nearly ten thousand organizations have successfully undergone the rigorous vetting process and earned the right to call themselves B Corps—including Unilever New Zealand, which we'll discuss in a later chapter, and Kickstarter. In a world where ESG goals were simply lip service, such a movement would struggle to get off the ground, as most organizations would be unwilling to meet such a high standard. Employees, investors, customers, suppliers, partners, and the market in general, however, have demonstrated a preference for working with, or for, organizations that are making a positive impact on the world, and this certification offers a high degree of credibility for making that claim. The four-day workweek has unsurprisingly proven popular among B Corps, as it helps them achieve some of their larger goals. "I actually had a call recently with a Bay Area nonprofit who was looking to pilot [the four-day workweek], and it was the first time I've talked to an employer that said, 'I feel like we need to do this, because so many other nonprofits in the Bay Area have adopted the framework,'" Jon says. "It's gotten to a tipping point within that sector in that community, but that's all you need to replicate it everywhere."

In 2011, at twenty-five years old, Grace Tallon became the youngest woman to ever sit on a county council in Dublin, but she couldn't imagine a long-term future in Irish politics for one simple reason.

"There was no maternity leave for women—it was only introduced in 2022—so at that stage, if a councillor went on maternity leave and they missed a meeting, they were marked as absent," she says. "Politicians can leave a room when a vote comes through if they strategically choose to abstain, and they're marked down the same way as a woman who is giving birth at that very moment."[16] Astute readers will recall that in 2018, coauthor Joe was conducting a study about work-life balance in Ireland's public sector, homing in on working parents—primarily women—who had taken a shorter workweek and accepted a lower salary but who were still as productive as their full-time colleagues. "When Joe was doing that survey, I was also thinking about how to even the playing field for women," Grace explains. "The shorter workweek is not a new concept; women have been doing it for years. They've been working a shorter week with the same responsibilities as their colleagues, except they're always apologizing for it and being made to feel guilty." Grace adds that this gender discrepancy isn't specific to working mothers, either. "Many are also looking after elderly parents, and those responsibilities generally do fall to women."

This need for greater flexibility adds a lot of anxiety and guilt to working women in the short term, but its greatest impacts are often felt on their careers over the long term. "They're going to be passed over for promotion opportunities because they're already working a shorter week," she says. "They also don't want to put themselves forward for leadership positions, because they have something else that they're trying to balance outside of work, or because they feel they're already getting some sort of extra benefit and don't feel confident asking for more."

Grace worked incredibly hard to reach public office at such a young age, but by 2019, she ultimately believed she could have either a successful career in politics or a family, but not both. "I never thought I would leave politics," she says. "I wanted to have a family, I didn't want to have to work really late, and the life of a politician doesn't really lend itself to that, and certainly not if you plan to take maternity leave." When she began considering her future family life back in 2011, the question was mostly theoretical. Soon after Grace decided not to run for reelection and to vacate her post in 2019, however, that future family started to become a little more real, because she had met Joe. Today, the pair live together—along with their two cocker spaniels—in Toronto.

After Grace left politics, she spent three years as the director of the Newpark Academy of Music in Dublin but eventually left to join her now life and business partner Joe as the global partnerships manager for 4 Day Week Global during his tenure as CEO and then as the chief operating officer (COO) of Work Time Revolution. There she also runs the organization's Women for Work Time Revolution initiative, aimed at supporting women who are working fewer hours. The initiative both advocates for a broader organizational program and provides assistance in developing strategies to get more done in less time.

For a brief period in 2020, Grace and other advocates of gender equality at work were hopeful that the switch to remote work would enable women to achieve meaningful work–life balance. Although flexible work ultimately makes it easier to manage home responsibilities, benefits of such policies are muted if the individual accommodation is not accompanied by greater collective workload management, as is often the case.

Flexibility policies, when offered on a voluntary basis as opposed to being implemented across the board, lead to a culture where those who take up the policy can be penalized for doing so, in what Hee-jung Chung calls the "flexibility paradox."[17] Grace explains that in an organization with more structural flexibility, where everyone is working four days, women can better manage their caregiving responsibilities without standing out from the rest of their team for having a unique schedule. The four-day schedule also forces organizations to pursue the work redesign effort that was often skipped in the sudden transition to remote work during the pandemic, ensuring a more thoughtful, collective approach. Furthermore, research from the pilot studies shows that men are more likely to take on more of those caregiving responsibilities after they adopt a shorter workweek themselves.

For example, in the UK pilot, men spent 27 percent more time looking after children once these workers moved to a four-day workweek, compared with women who spent 13 percent more time.

Furthermore, 60 percent of participants said the reduced schedule made it easier to balance work and home responsibilities. The day off from work also provided the opportunity to reduce day-care costs by 20 percent; these costs averaged nearly $11,600 per child per year in the United States in 2023, according to Child Care Aware of America.[18] That means that families with young children stand to gain around $2,320 per child while spending an extra day together each week. The trial participants with older children, meanwhile, said they could not overstate the value of having that time to themselves: a full day when the kids were in school each week, allowing them to take some much-needed and well-deserved time off from both work and home responsibilities to recharge.

Having a universal policy that does not single out women or pay them less for working fewer hours also makes it easier for women to make the changes required to do more in less time. That's because—as we'll discuss in more detail later in the book—there's only so much that employees can do on their own to find the efficiencies and to implement the time-saving strategies that make the four-day workweek possible. That effort becomes significantly easier when it's a shared goal rather than an individual responsibility.

———————

Our current workplace structure was designed and optimized for a single-breadwinner, single-homemaker household.

When the forty-hour workweek was codified in the Fair Labor Standards Act in 1940, only 28 percent of American women participated in the workforce, and single-parent families accounted for just 4 percent of US households.[19] Today, women account for 46.8 percent of the American workforce, and roughly one-quarter of American children live in a household with only one parent—typically their mother.[20] In the United States, 9 percent of women aged thirty-five to fifty-nine are single parents, compared with 2 percent of American men.

Although female workforce participation has skyrocketed in the last eighty-five years, women are still primarily responsible for domestic chores and caregiving. In fact, 59 percent of American women say they do most of the household chores, according to the Pew Research Center, compared with 6 percent of men.[21] Nearly half of the men surveyed say those responsibilities are shared evenly, but (perhaps unsurprisingly) most of the women disagree. While remote work was once considered a potential solution, data suggests it may have instead increased expectations on working women. Among households with two parents that can work remotely, women were much more likely to miss work to care for a sick child, according to a 2025 study conducted by researchers at the University of Southampton.[22] In it, 53 percent of working moms said they usually stay home when their child is sick, compared to 5 percent of dads. In fact, women with flexible work arrangement were 35 percent *less* likely to enjoy equal responsibility for sick days, in what is one of many demonstrations of Heejung Chung's "flexibility paradox" mentioned above.

As a result of these heightened expectations and responsibilities women are more likely to earn less, work fewer hours, and drop out of the workforce earlier. This disparity ultimately leaves employers with a smaller pool of female candidates for leadership positions. In 2023, full-time working women earned eighty-three cents for every dollar earned by their male counterparts in identical or similar roles.[23] Moreover, women were nearly twice as likely to work part-time.[24] That's not only true of American households, either. Across the member countries of the OECD, 21.5 percent of working-age women occupied part-time positions of less than thirty hours per week in 2021, compared with just 7.7 percent of men.

The challenges that exist for women to maintain full-time employment, advance their careers, and receive adequate compensation isn't just a problem for those women, or even their families. When women can't maintain a full-time role, they are less likely to be considered for advancement, and that lack of female leaders in the talent pipeline has a significant impact on business success. When McKinsey & Company began measuring the impact of gender-diverse leadership on business success in 2015, it found that companies in the top quartile for gender diversity on executive teams were 15 percent more likely to have financial returns above industry averages than those in the bottom quartile.[25] Each successive study into the effects of gender diversity on financial performance—including research conducted by McKinsey in 2018, 2020, and most recently in late 2023—found that gender-diverse leadership had an even greater impact over time. In its latest study, McKinsey found that companies in the top quartile for gender diversity had a 39 percent higher chance of outperforming those in the bottom quartile.[26]

The rise in female workforce participation has also been matched by a decline in birth rates across most Western nations, including the United States. As it becomes less feasible for a family to live on a single income, it becomes harder for both men and women to make the career and financial sacrifices necessary for parenthood. That is perhaps why American fertility rates have dropped precipitously over the last decade from a high of 69.3 births per thousand women aged fifteen to forty-four in 2017 to a record low of 54.4 in 2023, according to the American Centers for Disease Control and Prevention.[27] In the late 1970s, the US population grew at a rate of about 2 percent each year, but by the mid-1990s, population growth dipped below 1 percent. In 2023, the country grew at a rate of 0.8 percent per year, and the Bureau of Labor Statistics expects population growth to slow to 0.6 percent by 2033.

Declining birth rates, however, aren't just an American phenomenon. According to the World Bank, total births per woman have been falling for generations, from a high of 5.3 in 1963, to 3.3 by 1990, to just 2.3 in 2022, and that number is expected to decline in the years ahead. By 2050, three-quarters of countries are projected to dip below the replacement birth rate of 2.1 per woman, meaning that their native populations will be in decline.[28] By 2100, just six of the world's countries—three in Africa and three in the Pacific Islands—are expected to remain above the replacement rate. According to a 2024 OECD report, declining fertility rates—and with it, a declining global population—could pose "serious economic and social challenges" to future generations.[29]

In recent years, governments around the world have begun taking the issue more seriously and have found the four-day workweek to be a viable potential solution. After Japan's fertility rate hit a record low of 1.2 in 2023, for example, the country declared a national crisis.[30] In an effort to address the problem, the Tokyo Metropolitan Government implemented a four-day workweek for government employees, starting in April 2025. "We will review work styles . . . with flexibility, ensuring no one has to give up their career due to life events such as childbirth or childcare," said Tokyo governor Yuriko Koike when she unveiled the plan in late 2024. "Now is the time for Tokyo to take the initiative to protect and enhance the lives, livelihoods and economy of our people during these challenging times for the nation." In 2024, South Korea took a similar approach after declaring its declining fertility rate as a national emergency and one that the country concluded was largely the result of extreme working hours.[31] The Democratic Party of Korea even campaigned on a promise to reduce working hours from the current 40 per week to 36, with the stated goal of eventually achieving a four-day workweek, during an election it ultimately won in June of 2025.[32]

According to the pilot studies Joe coordinated, not only does the four-day workweek make it easier for women to balance their career and home lives, but it also encourages men to chip in more, while saving on childcare costs and allowing families to spend more time together. Perhaps the greatest impact, however, is in the workplace itself. By including caregivers with non-caregivers in the same companywide policy, those with greater responsibilities at home were more likely to be seen as equal contributors and more likely to be considered for advancement opportunities, rather than feeling singled out for their unique schedule. "Most of the research shows that you're evening the playing field, and you're making it a little bit easier for women to move up the ladder," Grace explains, adding she's seen this change in many of the companies she's worked with at Work Time Revolution. She adds that she has plenty of anecdotal data to suggest that four-day companies are more inclusive, but she's also hard at work trying to measure its effect.

"We're working with a number of academic partners to track women who have not reduced their work hours, women who have done so as an individual accommodation, and those who work at organizations that have introduced a reduced-hour schedule across the organization, and over the next few years, we'll be able to see the effects on each group," she says. "This career mobility piece, I think, is going to be really, really interesting. We'll monitor where and how they put themselves forward for leadership positions, as well as the other impacts it is having on their lives and careers."

The society that codified the forty-hour workweek looks a lot different from the one we have today. In purely mathematical terms, we might look at the old work schedule and suggest it's the same as the present one, but that conclusion ignores the reality that most households back then had only one working adult and another full-time caregiver. It also doesn't account for the reality that work is no longer constrained to formal working hours or spaces, due to both technological advancements and shifts in cultural expectation. In reality, total working hours among all household members have increased significantly, as the number of labor market participants has gone from one forty-hour worker to one and a half or two workers with much less stringent work-life boundaries. At the same time, the culture around who is primarily responsible for domestic responsibilities has not evolved in kind.

The four-day workweek offers many solutions to a lot of major business challenges, but some of its greatest gifts can only be viewed from a higher vantage point. A world of less work means a world of less emissions, more evenly balanced domestic responsibilities, more equitable workplaces, and more time spent with families, friends, and communities. The four-day workweek won't solve all of society's problems, but it can offer meaningful progress toward some of our greatest collective challenges through the proliferation of a significant personal benefit, not a significant personal sacrifice.

PART TWO

————

Doing More in Four

Proof in Practice

8 Redesigning Work for the Twenty-First Century

In 2020, Unilever New Zealand took a novel approach to a common set of business challenges, with incredible results.

The seventy-person subsidiary of the consumer product behemoth that's behind a laundry list of household consumer goods—including many actual laundry products—was facing a range of new challenges in the wake of the pandemic. Like many businesses at the time, staff were exhausted from a year of lockdowns, social distancing, and general disruptions to everyday life. In the four years leading up to the Covid-19 outbreak, Unilever New Zealand had enjoyed an incredible run, celebrating sixteen consecutive quarters of growth and becoming the global brand's most successful regional market in the process.

But as it emerged from what would sadly be just the first of many lockdowns in 2020, the company's then managing director, Cameron Heath, says the organization was facing the very real prospect of its first quarter of decline in years. "We had just been through a year of Covid lockdowns, we had just been through a period of change with a lot of disruption, a lot of additional pressure, and that caused a lot of fatigue among our people," he says, recalling all the new challenges brought by both the pandemic and the rapid transition to remote work—challenges like meeting and screen fatigue and increased care-giving responsibilities. "People were tired."[1]

Speaking from his home in Auckland, New Zealand, one sunny morning in the fall of 2024 (springtime here in North America), Cameron says the company was looking for a way to accelerate business performance in the wake of the pandemic. Those objectives included adding new technologies and processes that required some heavy lifting up front in the name of boosting productivity in the long term; avoiding the wave of resignations then sweeping the world as part of what would later be called the Great Resignation; and furthering the company's sustainability objectives. "We were looking for something that was impactful, that wasn't just . . . do the same as everyone else is doing, and hope for different results," he says. "The business had a really strong track record of performance and, through that, had generated a culture of experimentation, a culture of risk-taking, and a culture of doing things a little bit differently."

———————

When most businesses are concerned about employee productivity and performance, they ask their people to work more hours. Unilever New Zealand did the opposite.

In December 2020, the company began what was originally set to be a twelve-month trial—later expanded to eighteen months because of further pandemic-related disruptions—of a four-day workweek. During that time, staff were asked to complete 100 percent of their work in just 80 percent of the time, with no reduction in pay. Rather than prescribing a specific day off, staff were permitted to work with their managers to create their own thirty-two-hour schedule. Cameron says some chose to take off the same day every week, some preferred two half days, some ducked out a little earlier each day for five days, and others changed their schedule from week to week.

But making the switch wasn't as simple as telling everyone to go home (or, during the pandemic, to log off) early. Before initiating the four-day trial, Unilever implemented five major changes to its operations, which Cameron says were designed to ease the transition and increase its likelihood of success. Top of the list was manager engagement. "The number one person of influence on an employee's engagement, or the way in which they work, is their line manager," he says. "Bringing the line managers across our business on board to the concept early and really engaging them on how they lead for productivity through this concept of the four-day week was really important."

Second, the company beefed up its internal tech stack. The team worked with Microsoft to help its staff, as Microsoft put it, "work out loud" rather than in silos. That meant utilizing more tools for collaboration that provide managers and colleagues greater visibility into what others were up to, making it easier for staff to pick up where their colleagues had left off.

Third, the company had to completely revise its meeting culture. As experienced by many during the pandemic, the sudden switch from in-person to remote work had created a glut of unnecessary meetings that could have been an email. "We found that people were spending far, far too much time in meetings," Cameron explains. "Getting more disciplined and more focused on the way in which we use meetings in the business was really, really important."

The fourth major change that preceded the four-day workweek trial was a new set of employee training programs focused on work redesign. The programs were developed alongside Inventium, an Australian behavioral sciences business consulting firm and one of Joe's partners on the early pilots (Inventium happens to have its own four-day policy, which the company calls "the gift of the fifth"). Cameron adds that a transition of this magnitude would only be successful with enthusiastic employee buy-in.

"The last element that was critical to implementing the four-day week was probably just empowerment of our people," Cameron says. He explains that Unilever had no interest in—or ability to—make decisions on behalf of its staff, to decide for them which meetings were worth attending and which could be canceled, which days they should take off, or how to reprioritize their time to better focus on outcomes. "We said to people, 'With the tools that we've provided you, you're fully empowered to manage your diary, to manage the workflow, to push back and deprioritize where you don't believe that the work you're being asked to do is generating the right outcome or value for the business,'" he says.

One key distinction that Cameron often needs to explain to interested parties about the four-day week is that the extra time off is not equal to a vacation day or a typical weekend. Staff are still expected to pick up the phone when their clients or managers call and, when necessary, come in and work to meet deadlines or manage a work emergency on that fifth day. He adds that four days were intended to be the average but emphasizes that—as with any business—there are some weeks where the job requires extra time and others that have some to spare. "The business can be flexible in terms of allowing you to take that 20 percent of time when and where it suits you, but flexibility is a two-way street, and you need to demonstrate that flexibility back to the business," he says. "If the customer calls you on a Friday afternoon that you've got off, then you take the call—but usually it's only a ten-minute phone call, and when you hang up, you can continue your golf game or your time with family."

Though the four-day workweek was initiated as a specific solution to a specific challenge, Cameron has since come to realize that it represents something bigger; something badly needed in a world of increasing shareholder profits and a declining middle class, of rapidly advancing innovation and stubbornly stagnant wage growth, of more communication technology and less human connection. "Most businesses go through a two-year cycle, come up with a productivity exercise, cut head count, ask everyone to do a little bit more—to absorb additional workload and responsibility—and get nothing in return for it," he says. "For me the biggest differentiator in this approach is that there's a shared reward that is truly of value and meaning to the people that are giving the additional effort, the additional passion and energy into the business, and that shared reward is time."

Cameron is describing a common challenge that businesses have faced since at least the 1990s, when new operational efficiency programs were all the rage. Whether it's Lean, Six Sigma, Kaizen, or some other flavor-of-the-month management trend, many of these efficiency-enhancing strategies ultimately fail during implementation because they lack one vital ingredient: enthusiastic employee participation. If an employee's only reward for learning new skills and adopting new ways of doing things is more work or the opportunity to earn more money for shareholders, they're probably not going to make that transition easy for the company. Giving staff motivation to champion that effort by letting them share in the rewards is the most effective way to gain their support for broader organizational change—at least that was the theory. The question was whether it would hold up against business realities.

To answer that, Unilever invited the University of Technology Sydney to study the effects of the four-day workweek trial, which began in December 2020 and concluded eighteen months later, in June 2022. In November 2022, the researchers published their findings. Through those eighteen months, Unilever New Zealand continued its streak of revenue growth, adding six more quarters to its running total and delivering on every one of its business targets. When the researchers polled clients, they reported 100 percent satisfaction, with all agreeing the team completed its work on time and to a high standard. "At the end of the day, we're a customer service business," Cameron explains. "It was really important that we saw no disruption to the way in which those customers worked with us."

If you're wondering where staff found the hours to perform at such a high level, the data paints a clear picture of that too. The meeting reduction initiative alone cut meeting time by 3.5 hours per employee per week, and absenteeism dropped by 34 percent, thanks in part to a schedule that made it easier to book personal appointments, manage caretaking responsibilities, and handle other personal needs during the workweek. In fact, staff reported a 67 percent decrease in work-life conflicts. They also reported 33 percent lower levels of work-related stress and 15 percent more energy at work, meaning they were better equipped to maximize the hours they were on the clock. According to the analysis, 20 percent of staff used their day off primarily for personal chores, 18 percent used the day off to relax, 15 percent spent more time with friends and family, 15 percent spent more time exercising, and 11 percent used it as an opportunity to do more traveling.

"The business did perform better during the four-day workweek trial than it was performing previously, and it wasn't an underperforming business prior to the trial," Cameron says. "We had four years of consistent growth behind us already, but during the trial period, that growth accelerated." Not only did Unilever maintain the four-day schedule in New Zealand following the conclusion of its initial eighteen-month trial, but it also expanded the program to Unilever Australia's 600-person staff. "It's a larger business," says Cameron. "Larger revenue, larger head count, and it's a more complex business as well, because it has manufacturing sites. It has all of our logistics and supply chain teams, all of our marketing teams, and our sustainability team, so it's a much more complex part of our operation."

In early 2022, the Australian team began its four-day pilot program and, one year later, reported similar benefits, including reduced employee absenteeism and improved employee engagement, while continuing to achieve its revenue targets and other business objectives. According to Unilever Australia, employees reported significant improvements in work-life balance and engagement. Furthermore, the University of Technology Sydney confirmed that the trial was successful in driving greater efficiencies and productivity. In fact, every employee and business metric that was used to measure the success of the program either remained stable or showed improvement.

Despite its success, however, Cameron doesn't believe that Unilever will soon spread the policy across its 180,000 employees in 150 countries. Like many global enterprises, Unilever maintains a high degree of autonomy across its many functions and jurisdictions, rather than mandating a one-size-fits-all policy. And like most of the larger, more complex organizations Joe has worked with in recent years, Unilever is taking an experimental rather than universal approach to the four-day workweek too. Should market adoption of the four-day workweek ramp up in the years ahead, the enterprises that have not only explored the concept but also successfully tested it in parts of their operations will be well positioned to scale up more quickly and smoothly than their competitors. "The trial has brought about so many learnings and insights around flexibility—and those learnings and insights can be and have been applied in different ways around the world—but I don't think that there's an appetite to take a blanket approach globally," Cameron says. If Unilever ever does decide to expand the program, however, it will have the benefit of an internal playbook developed by its business units in New Zealand and Australia.

In the meantime, both Unilever offices continue to operate on a four-day schedule more than five years after New Zealand made the switch and three years after Australia did so, and Cameron says they're continuing to enjoy the benefits, because they continue to put in the work. He explains that when done right, the four-day week becomes a self-reinforcing mechanism, encouraging staff to continue seeking ways to get more done in less time to maintain what has been, for many, a life-changing workplace benefit.

When we spoke with Cameron in mid-2024, Unilever New Zealand was on its twenty-fifth quarter of consecutive growth, spanning more than six years, half of which have been under a reduced schedule.

———————————

Unilever is one of many organizations that used the disruption of the Covid-19 pandemic to reevaluate whether the way things had always been done still suited their current and future needs and ultimately determined it did not.

The pandemic didn't change the feasibility of doing things differently; it merely provided the necessary opportunity to reevaluate whether the "way it's always been done" is still the best way forward. For leaders and organizations bold enough to ask the question, the answer was often a resounding "no." Like remote work, a four-day workweek was feasible for large sections of the workforce long before the pandemic arrived. As we noted in previous chapters, there were isolated experiments proving so, long before the spring of 2020.

When Jared kick-started his career as a freelance journalist in 2013, he joined a small club of people who worked remotely full-time. While about 23 percent of the population did some of their work remotely back then, just three million Americans—less than 1 percent of the population—worked exclusively from home.[2] At the time, this was less of a choice than a necessity. The then twenty-five-year-old couldn't afford a formal workspace, so he squeezed a tiny IKEA desk into the corner of his one-bedroom apartment and began building his writing business. Much to his surprise, Jared absolutely loved working remotely. He got to sleep in a little later, saved time and money on commuting, did his laundry or minor errands throughout the day, and wore whatever made him most comfortable at work (at least on his bottom half).

Within a few months of working remotely, Jared determined that he could never go back to working in an office full-time. This realization is now shared by many, but at the time, he felt entirely alone in that sentiment. As he spoke to friends, colleagues, and family about how much he enjoyed remote work—how much more productive he was, how much time and money he was saving—people often responded with some version of "that's good for you, but it just wouldn't work for me." In these conversations, folks would say that remote work didn't suit the kind of work they did, their industry, their company culture, or their personal preferences. Of course, none had tried working remotely, but as soon as they imagined a different way of doing things, they immediately considered the potential challenges, ignored the potential upside, and abandoned the idea. The more he talked to others about how great it was to work remotely, the more Jared was convinced there was something unique about him, his working style, or his relationship with work. Of course we now know that a lot of people want to work remotely—as much as 98 percent of knowledge workers, according to one survey conducted in 2013.[3] But back in 2013, Jared was convinced he was unique or odd or both (the jury is still out).

Remember, this was back in 2013, before Slack had launched to the public and before Zoom and Teams were common workplace tools. Jared fell in love with remote work before remote work was even convenient or enabled by all the new platforms and technologies that have become available since the pandemic. Of course, you know where we're going with this; the more Jared reported on the four-day workweek, the more he saw the parallels. "That's good for you, but I could never imagine it working for me." As he heard many times in regard to working remotely, folks still say it doesn't suit the kind of work they do, their industry, their workplace culture, or their personal preferences. None of these folks have tried it, but as soon as they try to picture a different way of doing things, they immediately consider the potential challenges, ignore the potential upside, and abandon the possibility. Humans hate change. We're built to pursue stability, consistency, and predictability, and the five-day standard neatly represents all those things. Maintaining the status quo is easier than changing, even when the status quo has long outgrown its necessity.

The pandemic forced people to finally try what Jared had been raving about for the better part of a decade. Once the initial challenges of the pandemic wore down and people got to enjoy working from home without their kids in the next room, or disinfecting their groceries, or watching a wave of constant doom and gloom on the news, most refused to switch back. It was a strange path to vindication, but vindication nonetheless. Now many of those same doubters Jared interacted with when he began working remotely are fighting their own employers for the right to continue doing so themselves. Let's hope it doesn't take another event as tragic and devastating as a pandemic for the world to recognize the merits of a four-day workweek.

Now, when Jared speaks to others about the four-day week and receives the same "it's good for you but could never work for me" response, he thinks back to those days when he started working remotely. He remembers his cozy sweatpants, his little IKEA desk, and staring out the window of his one-bedroom apartment, watching the shivering strangers shuffling through the snow on their morning commute, and grinning at the thought of being freed from their misery—only this time, he's fairly certain he's not unique or odd.

When anyone asks about the four-day workweek, Simon Ursell, the founder and chair of environmental planning service Tyler Grange, likes to tell the story of the Guru and the Cat.

The fable goes something like this: Every evening, the guru leads his disciples in prayer at an ashram (or monastery) in India. One day a cat showed up to the ashram, and when the guru sat down to worship, the cat's meowing and whining became a distraction. After trying and failing to ignore the feline intruder, the guru ordered that the cat be tied up out of sight and meowing distance of his worshippers before prayer and freed immediately after. Despite being bound that first night, the cat returned the next evening, purring and meowing loud enough to take attention away from prayer and forcing the guru to issue the same instructions. And so the ritual continued night after night, with the guru delaying prayer until the cat was sufficiently dealt with.

After many years of this practice, the guru passed away, but the cat remained, and so the worshippers continued the ritual of temporarily ridding themselves of the distraction. More years passed, and eventually the cat expired too. That's when the worshippers brought another cat to the ashram to continue the practice. Decades later, the descendants of the guru's original disciples spent endless hours gathering around the ashram, debating the liturgical significance of tying up a cat during worship. "I think the five-day week is a guru's cat," says Simon from his home in the English countryside. "We do it because we've always done it, and because everyone else is doing it; we've given it a mythical significance."[4]

When Simon created Tyler Grange in London in 2009, he and his cofounders decided to give the staff of their environmental consultancy one day off each month to volunteer. A few years later, Simon read an article about the four-day workweek but didn't think much about it. That is until one fateful night when Simon awoke in a cold sweat. "I had a nightmare that one of our close competitors had already done it, that they'd announced it," he says, adding that the dream caused him to curse aloud from his bed in the middle of the night. "I realized at that moment the benefit of us being a four-day week early adopter, to acting now."

Those benefits, he says, include media coverage for his firm—a perk which he suggests inclusion in this book and countless other media appearances have fully validated—and the ability to recruit more competitively. Both advantages, he feared in his dream and on waking, would be diminished once the concept became more mainstream. After Simon spent a few months thinking it over with his colleagues and consulting with Joe, Tyler Grange signed up to be one of the sixty-one organizations that participated in the UK four-day workweek trial, which began in the summer of 2022.

"When we implemented a four-day week, we got rid of the monthly volunteer day, but everybody in the business agreed—and we wrote it into all our employment contracts—that you have to volunteer if you're part of Tyler Grange," he says, adding that working parents are exempt.

Simon realized that, like Unilever, Tyler Grange would also have to find enough efficiencies in its processes to enable its people to do the same, or more, in less time. That meant onboarding a range of new digital solutions, formalizing processes that had long been ad hoc, and ruthlessly cutting down on time spent in meetings. What his staff didn't know at the time, however, was that these were steps Simon and his leadership team had wanted to take for a long time. Prior to implementing the four-day workweek, they had mapped out the many ways in which their business had to evolve, and they were stuck on the challenge of getting sufficient employee buy-in to successfully pursue big and often-disruptive changes. By adding the incentive of a four-day workweek, he says, he was able to pursue a series of bold updates to business operations—changes that would have been unsuccessful otherwise. "If I tried to push those changes through into the five-day Tyler Grange business, we would have probably lost a third of the team, if not half, because change is hard, it's painful, it requires a lot of effort," he says. "The wonderful thing about a four-day week is it is just the best incentive. If you're saying the reason we want the change is to allow you to have a better lifestyle, they'll say, 'Hell yeah. How can I help?'"

Not every pilot participant engaged in a ruthless optimization campaign before making the switch. On the day the trial was set to begin, all sixty-one participants gathered on Zoom, and Simon noticed that one person had a large pile of balloons in the background. "They said, 'As soon as we're off this call, we're going to tell our team,' and there was a silence around the room, because we had all spoken to our teams for months—in our case six months, and some even longer—before that, so we all kind of knew how that would go, which is not well." As Simon anticipated that unnamed company was one of the five that ultimately didn't succeed in making the transition permanent after the trial ended, proving the importance of employee engagement and proper planning.

Tyler Grange, meanwhile, saw immediate improvements in its overall business outcomes during the trial period, including a 30 percent jump in overall productivity and a significant boost to recruitment, retention, and engagement. More than two years after implementing a shorter workweek, Simon is more confident than ever that the company will only continue to grow, because his team remains motivated to continually find greater efficiencies. "The numbers are still getting better, we're getting more productive, because we've got a culture focused on productivity, and we're always looking for ways to be more productive," he says, adding that the policy, which has been in place since the trial, has also provided an ongoing recruiting advantage. "If you want to recruit the very best people, go to a four-day week—and if you recruit the very best people, you're going to be the best. I mean, I think that's pretty obvious."

As for financial performance, Simon doesn't like to talk about money, given that Tyler Grange is a B Corp focused on helping clients improve their environmental sustainability. At the same time, he's happy to share that the cottage from which he relayed his story, in central England, is just down the street from Princess Anne's home, near the pub that was once frequented by Princes Harry and William. As we spoke, King Charles was staying at his royal residence about a mile away. While Simon insists he isn't motivated by money, he concedes that he's made a lot of it, which he credits to making decisions that are not motivated by money. "Culture eats profit for breakfast," he says. "If your business has a very strong sense of purpose and a really clear way of doing things, it's going to be successful." Simon says he owes Tyler Grange's success to the quality of his staff, which he in turn owes to his leadership team's willingness to question longstanding norms and seek better ways of doing things. The lesson: put away the rope, let the cat roam free, and you could be the only monastery in the region not spending hours chasing felines and debating the meaning of an entirely pointless activity.

9 An Antidote to Hustle Culture

When Leena Yousefi began her career in family law, she explicitly wanted to work for the kind of pull-no-punches firm that doesn't give a damn about your sleep schedule, your family life, or your personal wellness journey.

"After I graduated, I had a lovely job as an articling student at a small firm in North Vancouver, but it just wasn't enough," she says. "I wanted to go work for a shark; I wanted to work my ass off. I wanted to overwork myself. I was determined to basically become a pro at it."[1]

Leena wasn't always that ambitious. In fact, in 2002 she was expelled from the University of Victoria for failing to show up to class. The Iranian immigrant's parents—a professor and an architect—had left the war-torn state to raise their two daughters in a country that would give them a real chance to make a life for themselves, but the transition proved difficult at first. "The combination of childhood trauma and also emigrating to Canada during my teenage years resulted in me not performing well at university due to depression, and I was eventually expelled because of that," Leena says. "I was basically drifting, smoking a lot of pot, and one day the same pain that had made me want to be numb to the world kind of jolted me into wanting to be perfect and achieve everything that I could to be very successful." Once that switch was flipped in her mind, Leena says nothing could stop her.

Two years after dropping out of school, she returned to the University of Victoria, where she earned straight As, gaining acceptance to eleven of the twelve law schools she applied to. So, when she finally graduated and entered the workforce in 2010, Leena says she had no patience for the feel-good, highly principled, work-life-balancing family law firm that first hired her in North Vancouver; she wanted to swim with the sharks. "I left that job and took on a very demanding job at a medium-sized law firm in downtown Vancouver," she says. "I worked with sharks, and it was awesome. I got what I wanted, I gained experience, I became a very good lawyer, and I was kind of in that scene."

At first, Leena loved the long hours and bullshit-free work environment, but two years later, she says, things started to change. Leena explains that family law is itself one of the most emotionally taxing jobs for legal professionals—an industry already prone to highly stressful working conditions—and as the years went on, the work started to take an emotional toll. "Divorce has been proven to be the second most stressful thing that any person can go through after the loss of a child," she says. "So if you deal with that every day for a living, the last thing you need is a negative work environment. Your work environment needs to be calm and positive and supportive." Unfortunately, Leena's employer chose to go in the opposite direction.

In 2012, the growing firm hired a new COO, who was tasked with squeezing every ounce of productivity out of the staff, and the workplace quickly shifted from demanding to outright toxic. "The wrong person was hired," she says, matter-of-factly. "She had a lot of jealousy and animosity against other—mostly female—lawyers, and she created a ton of division. We couldn't focus on our clients or our files; it became a civil war at the firm." At first Leena did what she had always done and pushed through the pain, but eventually the stress and anxiety became impossible to ignore. "I started having really bad migraines, and on the advice of my doctor, I was told to work four days a week," she says.

That suggestion wasn't taken at face value by her new manager, who forced her to leave the office immediately and speak with another medical professional to gain a second opinion. After that doctor made the same recommendation, Leena's employer was obligated to take the issue seriously or otherwise risk significant liability. "They couldn't say 'no,' because it was a medical issue, but immediately they cut my pay by 20 percent, and obviously the reaction definitely was not supportive." Leena says that the math made sense, at least on paper; she would work 20 percent less, and her employer thought it only fair to pay her 20 percent less, in expectation of an equal-sized drop in her billable hours. However, after switching to a four-day workweek, Leena continued to accomplish as much as she had on a full-time schedule. "I kept on meeting the target, and I also felt really good and healthy and happy," she says. "That feeling of having Fridays off and not having to be anywhere, and at the same time serving my clients and meeting my targets, was a surprise to me and it was a surprise to my employer."

Though Leena was finally enjoying a degree of work-life balance, her colleagues were still struggling under their new COO and began exiting the firm, prompting Leena to reevaluate her own employment situation. "At that point, I had a choice: to go and work for another law firm or go out on my own," she says. "I was really young, very junior—I only had two years of experience. I was very scared, but I think I just didn't have the stamina to go out and look for another workplace and deal with the same toxic culture drama issues." In January 2013, Leena tendered her resignation.

Leena's mental health challenges are, sadly, more the norm than the exception in the legal profession. Not only does the job typically require long hours, but it also requires dealing with difficult circumstances—be they divorce, disputes, or criminality. The high-stakes nature of the work, the high demands put on its practitioners, the long hours they're often expected to log—and, for many, a culture of suppressing or ignoring mental health issues—all contribute to higher-than-average rates of loneliness, anxiety, depression, burnout, substance abuse, and suicide.

A 2023 study of two thousand lawyers in California and Washington, DC, for example, found that legal professionals were twice as likely to have suicidal thoughts than other working Americans, with 8.5 percent of respondents admitting to contemplating hurting themselves or committing suicide.[2] Unsurprisingly, the lawyers under the most pressure displayed the greatest mental health distress. Those who complained of "high work commitments" were 2.2 times more likely to have suicidal thoughts and 2.8 times more likely to struggle with loneliness. Among those who said they were struggling, 66 percent said their profession had been detrimental to their mental health and 46 percent said they were considering leaving the industry because of stress and burnout.

The study also found a direct connection between hours worked per week and thoughts of suicide. According to the study, roughly 8 percent of legal professionals who worked 31 to 50 hours each week had thoughts of suicide, compared with 9.1 percent of those who worked 51 to 60 hours a week and nearly 15 percent of those who worked 61 to 70 hours a week. While the sources of stress were many, nearly half of judges surveyed said that dealing with contentious family law issues was a major contributor to their mental health challenges.

Across jurisdictions, legal professionals consistently report mental health challenges at higher rates. In a 2022 study of seventy-three hundred Canadian legal professionals, 57.5 percent reported high levels of psychological distress. According to the study, nearly one in four had suicidal thoughts after they started working in the field, while 35.7 percent experienced high levels of anxiety.[3]

But of course, lawyers aren't alone in feeling overworked and overwhelmed by their jobs. In fact, a 2024 survey of twelve thousand professionals by Mercer found that 82 percent of the workforce is at high risk of burnout because of excessive workload, exhaustion, and financial strain.[4]

Three weeks after quitting her job, Leena opened her own firm, YLaw, in a modest shared office space before upgrading to the upscale cobblestoned neighborhood of Yaletown in Vancouver three years later. There she remains nestled between tech company headquarters, cocktail bars, and trendy cafés, just a pebble's throw from the Pacific Ocean.

Despite trading her four-day schedule for the round-the-clock demands of running her own firm, Leena says she had never been happier at work. "The migraines went away," she says. "The job itself obviously was and continues to be very difficult, but that work environment really pushed me forward. I was working a lot more, but I was happy. I wasn't even tired. It was lovely." For the first four years as both business owner and lawyer, Leena says she did everything herself, including building and managing her website, signing new clients, and attending hearings. Eventually, however, the company grew too big to manage on her own. "After four years, the ball really started rolling," she says. "We had more clients than we could handle, so I started hiring more lawyers, and before we knew it, we just expanded exponentially. In five years, we grew by more than 500 percent and we became one of the fastest growing companies in the country."

As the firm grew bigger, Leena once again found herself working around the clock, not by choice but by necessity, and soon the panic attacks and migraines crept back into her life. "I was doing two court hearings a day, five days a week, and working seven days a week. It was very difficult," she says. Fearing for her own well-being, Leena decided to reduce her caseload and focus her energy on running the business, but admits that she continued working similar hours, albeit on less emotionally taxing tasks.

It wasn't until she had her first child in 2017 that Leena says she took a meaningful step away from work. After her daughter was born, she returned to work a couple of days each week, then added a third and then a fourth, but never fully returned to a five-day schedule. "I had worked myself up to four days a week, and I started really enjoying that, and I saw that I was once again basically doing what I was doing when I was working five days a week," she says. "And then one night as I was cooking dinner, an idea popped into my head: Why not do this for everybody else and see how it goes?"

Having worked for companies that demanded too little, and too much, Leena was keen to build the firm that found the Goldilocks zone of productivity. She decided that she was willing to gamble 10 percent of the firm's profits on cutting 10 percent of its hours and switching to a four-day schedule of nine hours per day. Though nine hours may seem like a long workday to some, it's still relatively short in the legal industry (and in some of its most demanding corners, it's almost a half day). "I basically just asked my people, 'What day would you like to have off?' and the majority vote was Wednesdays," she says. "So we planned it out so that most of the staff would be off on Wednesday, and we would have one receptionist, one assistant, and one lawyer on call." Leena adds that when she surveyed the staff recently, most admitted to working an hour or two on most Wednesdays—a practice she says is still within the spirit of the policy. "That's perfectly fine," she says. "The benefit is the psychological autonomy and freedom of not having to clock in and clock out—it's their call."

The switch also required some minor adjustments to other workplace policies. For example, Leena had to change the language of YLaw's employment contracts to specify that weeks with a statutory holiday didn't switch to three days but that the Wednesday day off would be instead replaced with the holiday. She also had to adjust the language of her time-off allowance from specifying how many days staff could take off to how many weeks. In other words, the former four weeks' worth of vacation now equated to sixteen paid vacation days, not the twenty that had been offered in the previous five-day schedule. Once those details were ironed out, YLaw kicked off a three-month trial of the new schedule, starting in March 2021.

Though YLaw didn't dramatically change its underlying work structures, Leena says the firm was already ahead of the industry in that regard, as it had recently adopted new tools and systems in its transition to remote and hybrid work during the pandemic. "We were probably already in the top twentieth percentile for using technology at a law firm, but that's because some firms are still using pen and paper to schedule things," she says. For example, the company had recently adopted a new system that enabled greater information sharing and knowledge management in a more remote and hybrid setting. "We started limiting our meetings, for example," she says. "We started using messaging instead of emails to be more efficient, and we started doing a lot of procedural stuff differently—like we use AI for statistical gathering."

_____

Despite reducing her staff's working hours and billable targets by 10 percent, Leena says she didn't make any changes to their compensation.

Before the four-day trial began, staff were expected to hit a billable-hour target of 1,500 per year, equivalent to roughly 35 hours a week. But after switching to the four-day schedule, they were only responsible for 1,400 hours per year. Leena says her team has managed to maintain that target, and much to her surprise some have even continued to hit 1,500. "They're not billing more than they did working five days a week, that's for sure, but they're not necessarily billing less, either." Over the next eighteen months, the company doubled in size, becoming British Columbia's fastest growing firm in the process. Nearly five years later, YLaw, which now boasts three locations and a team of twenty-five lawyers, continues to operate on that same four-day schedule of nine hours per day. "Our turnover is almost zero," Leena says. "We've only had one person leave to go to another law firm since we implemented this. They say they can't imagine working anywhere else for five days a week. Even if the enthusiasm does fade, it's the expectation and the lifestyle that they're no longer willing to let go of."

There was only one unintended negative consequence that Leena later had to correct. After YLaw switched to a four-day workweek, it received a huge spike in candidate applications, but Leena says not all of them were applying for the right reasons. "We do sometimes get applicants that confuse this policy with permission to be lazy—they apply because they're lazy, not because they want to be healthy," she says. In response, Leena implemented a probationary period prior to extending the benefit to new hires. At the same time, Leena says she also gets a lot of applications from lawyers at the other end of the talent spectrum. "We've gotten applicants that we never imagined getting in a million years. A lot of senior lawyers don't want to be under so much pressure and just want an environment where we still work very hard but it's a little bit more relaxed and not as stressful. So that's been a really nice side effect as well."

Leena says the experiment also revealed an underlying truth about the legal industry as a whole: that the billable-hour targets of major law firms are simply not sustainable in the long run. "These are targets that an associate may be able to meet—most associates, anyway—for the first three to five years, but then either they burn out or they leave the firm, and they go to try to find another job where the targets are not so extreme," she says, adding that many expect eighteen hundred to twenty-one hundred per year. "We had a very reasonable target to begin with." Leena explains that the big firms with unrealistic and unsustainable targets will never be able to maintain their business on a reduced schedule, but they also won't be able to hang on to their most talented staff for very long, either. Eventually, most staff will end up burning out, quitting, or both. She does, however, believe that any firm with realistic and sustainable expectations should be able to switch to a four-day workweek without suffering any financial losses in the process.

For those keeping track at home, YLaw's staff typically work a thirty-six-hour weekly schedule (nine hours for four days), plus one or two more hours when needed on Wednesday.

They also have a few less vacation days (but the same amount of vacation weeks), and there is effectively no change to their schedule on the eleven weeks that the province of British Columbia celebrates statutory holidays each year.[5] When you add it all up, you get almost the same annual work schedule as a typical company with a summer Friday policy.

In exchange, YLaw has been able to recruit some of the industry's top talent and has found an effective solution for the anxiety, depression, burnout, and other mental health challenges that plague the entire industry—and especially the family law practice. As the kids would say, the math is "mathing."

After being nearly pushed out of the industry because of its impossibly high demands, Leena has proven the viability of a four-day model at a small firm—and then, thanks to YLaw's growth, a medium-sized firm, but she isn't stopping there. "We want to become a big law firm, so that we can go head-to-head with other major firms and show them that this can work, and it can be sustainable, profitable, successful, and a new model of running a firm, even on a big scale," she says. "First, they laughed, and now they're quiet and watching, but I'm hoping one day in the future, they're going to follow. That would be my purpose."

A decade and a half after graduating with nothing but ambition, Leena says she has learned a valuable lesson about what it takes to be the best in a highly competitive field. Too much hard work doesn't lead to success and fortune as often as it leads to dissatisfaction, disengagement, and burnout. If you're not careful, the relentless pursuit of productivity can quickly turn into a productivity killer. That's especially true in high-pressure industries where, like in the legal field, workers enter with the expectation that they will be worked to the bone.

Leena always wanted to push herself and her team to their limit—it just took a few years to learn that getting the most out of herself and her staff required less work time, not more. "I was working towards that goal just like a pro athlete or pro piano player—you don't do a nine-to-five to become pro," she says. "As you get older, and you become wiser you realize you can't sustain this. . . . That's why I think that this is a formula that, regardless of how good you want to be at what you want to do, you can still work less and achieve the same goal and avoid burning out before you get there."

10 A Catalyst for Creativity

There's a reason why our best thinking seldom happens in a sterile workplace or under a tight deadline or in times of high emotion or stress.

Instead, research has found that our greatest opportunities for creativity occur when our mind has open space to wander, like in the shower, on a long walk, or in bed late at night. That's because, according to psychologists, intense cognitive effort changes our biochemistry in ways that make it nearly impossible to get into a flow state or achieve deep thought.[1] When those stress hormones are activated, our brains go into flight-or-flight mode, providing a sudden burst of energy, expanding our airways, and sending extra oxygen to the brain to increase alertness.[2] This stress response primes our brains to focus on surviving some kind of immediate danger, which is great if you're about to fight a bear but not so great if you're trying to come up with a new marketing campaign before a deadline.

While much remains unknown about the creative process, researchers can conclude with some degree of confidence that the brain is best able to find novel and creative ideas when it's relaxed, unconstrained by outside pressure, and able to roam free. According to the research, engaging in very light activities that are part of a typical routine—like showering, folding laundry, or mowing the lawn—puts the brain into a sort of autopilot mode in the physical world, creating an ideal scenario for creative thought.[3] That's why we naturally shut our eyes or stare at the floor or ceiling when we're trying to concentrate; that's our brain's way of trying to shut out distractions. It's something University of Virginia researchers have dubbed "the shower effect," leading them to conclude that mildly engaging tasks can produce the greatest creative outputs.[4] Sometimes, not trying to solve work problems enables us to dream up the most innovative solutions.

Ironic, then, that we have historically put creative professionals to work in settings that are the least conducive to free-flowing thought—busy workplaces rife with personal agendas and politics, deadlines and deliverables, buzzing devices and distractions. If we really want to get the most out of creatives, we should encourage them to spend more of their time doing things that let their brains cruise on autopilot. That is ultimately what Daly did, albeit unintentionally.

———————

Founded in New York City's trendy SoHo neighborhood in 2019, the communications and marketing agency has been fully remote since the pandemic began soon after.

Founder Alex Daly is now based in Miami, managing director Ally Bruschi works three time zones away in Los Angeles, while the rest of the eleven-person staff are spread across the country—and even across the globe, in the case of a few team members who have adopted the digital nomad lifestyle. As was the case for many businesses, 2020 proved to be a particularly difficult year for Daly. The widespread economic uncertainty that accompanied the outbreak of the pandemic resulted in a lot of lost business and much anxiety among the staff regarding their own job security. To make matters worse, by the summer of 2020, New York City had become the epicenter of the global health crisis. "It was such a turbulent, tough time, not only financially and economically. There was a lot happening in the news cycle, a lot of pain, a lot of stress, but we really didn't want to approach this time with a lens of scarcity," Alex says, explaining that she didn't need her already-stressed-out and thinly spread staff worrying about job security.[5]

"Especially in 2020, we saw our team get incredibly burnt out," adds Ally. "It was just a really uncertain and hard year, I think, for Alex as a founder, me as a leader, and really for our whole team, even down to our interns."

When the company was founded in 2019, Alex gave her first employee, Ally—and all subsequent hires—permission to duck out at 3 p.m. on Fridays in June, July, and August. As the pandemic went from bad to worse, they extended the summer Friday schedule through the year in hopes that it would offer their team some relief, as part of a program they called Forever Summer Fridays. "It's not like we could give our team more money to take care of themselves; we just didn't have it," Alex explains. "So, we were trying to find ways to offer substantive value through benefits that wouldn't actually be costly."

Daly ultimately maintained the reduced Friday schedule through the remainder of 2021, and the program received a lot of positive feedback from staff without presenting any negative side effects. In fact, the team members were more upbeat, positive, and ultimately effective at work, despite working fewer hours.

Following the success of their Forever Summer Fridays trial, Alex and Ally wanted to explore ways to take the concept a step further. As they started doing their research, the two discovered some of the promising data from Joe's pilot programs and began attending some of his information sessions, though they still had some reservations about taking Fridays off entirely. "Something that was really sticking with us throughout 2022 was that we heard about all the successful case studies and stories of companies that were doing the four-day workweek really well—how it was great for worker mental health without sacrificing productivity," Ally says. "But we weren't really hearing that perspective from client-facing companies, like communications, marketing, and design agencies like ourselves." In 2022, Alex and Ally say they "cobbled together" a bunch of ideas from a variety of sources and designed a shorter workweek that was unique to their organization.

"We came up with a way to still have coverage across all five days," Ally says. "The full team is working each of the five days of the traditional workweek, but we kept the early dismissals on Friday, implemented a late start on Mondays, and then shaved off the last thirty minutes of every other workday to get to a thirty-two-hour workweek. We piloted that in 2023, called it a trial of what we labeled 'Slowdown Time,' and we invited feedback or ideas or thoughts from the team. I don't know any teams that do the four-day workweek like we do."

While most organizations make sweeping changes to their internal operations to find those extra hours, Alex and Ally admit to doing very little preparation before switching to their new schedule. That's in part because the team had already been operating on a slightly reduced schedule with its Forever Summer Fridays for several years and because Alex and Ally say they tend to hire staff they can trust. "I wasn't really worried," Alex says. "We really had done so much of the groundwork for this to succeed in terms of our operations and our culture, so it didn't seem scary to us. A big part of it too is that we trust our team, inherently. We really trust that they're aiming to do their best work, and with that we can trust them to manage their own time. So, we didn't have to be monitoring our team; we knew that they would get it done and do it well."

While the idea of reducing working hours was initially introduced as a way to address burnout, anxiety, and other mental health challenges during the pandemic, Alex and Ally began to notice other benefits that they hadn't anticipated. "You can't squeeze every last drop of productivity out of someone's creative brain—people need to bring their most productive selves to the workplace," Alex suggests. "In our industry, you really do need to give people the space to rest and recharge and come to the workday with their best self and brain, and you don't get that by having people work eighty-hour weeks and not taking vacations. It just doesn't work that way." Alex says that as the company reduced its working hours, its staff seemed to generate more ideas and more creative solutions, especially during the parts of the week that they were no longer technically on the clock. "We have found that if we can shorten our workweek and give people some of their time back, we can still deliver excellent client work—maybe even better client work than we were doing before—because people have that time and space."

Thus far we've heard from four organizations with four entirely different approaches to the four-day workweek, and that's no accident.

Like most innovative workplace policies, the four-day workweek is more of a framework than a prescription. For some firms—particularly those with more project-based work and whose employees generate most of their value through internal collaboration—it makes sense to have a single organization-wide day off. For those that must maintain service coverage for clients across five days, a roster or a shift-based arrangement will probably prove more beneficial. When designing your four-day workweek, ask yourself which is more critical for success: maximizing availability to each other or to clients and external stakeholders. While some companies, like Unilever New Zealand, are in a position to enable their staff to pick and choose their own weekly schedules, others, like YLaw and Tyler Grange, will find it easier or more beneficial to keep everyone on the same schedule, whether that means taking off Wednesdays or Fridays. Others still, like Daly, will discover that the best solution for them is not a full day off but a little less work time during what are generally their least productive hours. We've shared these stories with you to demonstrate the diversity of approaches that still embody the same spirit of the four-day movement. In fact, if we really wanted to get technical, we would call it *work time reduction*, rather than the *four-day workweek* (though it doesn't really have the same ring to it).

───────────

After implementing the shortened schedule, Daly's communications director, Hailey Murphy, says that her clients hardly even noticed the switch, though it made a significant impact on her life.

"I was worried about how our clients would react, what they would think, and if they would feel like they weren't getting enough attention," she says. "It has never once come up."[6] Hailey suspects that the reason has a lot to do with Alex and Ally's unique schedule reduction strategy. "Something I have always known from my dad who worked in corporate America is that there is BS time in the week—namely, Monday mornings and Friday afternoons—when you're not actually doing anything; you're just getting on your computer, kind of messing around, because you have to be there," she says. Instead of "messing around" during those hours, Hailey says she's been able to take care of most of her weekly household chores, leaving Saturdays and Sundays open for some actual time off. "I'll go to the grocery store or mop my floors or do some laundry—this past Monday, I went to the tailor to get a dress tailored—and it sounds silly, but to not have the pressure to do that on weekends feels very nice."

Since Daly switched to the reduced schedule, Hailey says she also escaped the weekly rush of anxiety experienced by many working adults at the end of the weekend—a feeling known as the Sunday Scaries. "My husband will often look at me on Sunday night when his [scaries] are hitting and say, 'You don't have to work in the morning,' and I say, 'No, I don't,'" she says with a smile. "It's hard to describe the kind of anxiety that's relieved solely by not having to be on a computer at nine a.m. Monday."

Although Monday mornings are typically spent tackling household chores, the thirty-one-year-old Jersey City, New Jersey, resident says she still reserves her Friday afternoons for fun activities. She might beat the traffic ahead of a weekend getaway or make appointments with a Manhattan acupuncturist who is typically booked solid on evenings and weekends. Ironically, the costs of these significant life improvements are not really costs at all. Hailey says her clients rarely reach out on Monday mornings or Friday afternoons, and when they do, she's usually able to address their needs quickly before getting back to whatever activity she was enjoying previously.

The Slowdown Time schedule wasn't just a nice change of pace from Hailey's previous experience at Daly but also an even greater change from her previous experience in the communications industry. Prior to Daly, Hailey worked as an in-house communications professional for a major news organization that had no real limits on work hours. "Public relations is a career where you have to be available at all times," she says. "At any moment, the company you work for or the client you work with could go through an emergency, and you have to drop everything and support them, and that's happened so many more times than I can tell you." Canceling plans last minute, cutting trips short, and coming in early or staying late when duty called was more the norm than the exception during the earlier part of Hailey's career. Those expectations are partly what drove her to work for Daly, which is less prone to time-sensitive emergencies and whose leadership team (namely, Alex and Ally) make a conscious effort to let their staff enjoy their time away from work worry-free.

Hailey's prior experience, however, does speak to a reality of modern work that makes time off even more valuable. Just twenty years ago, most knowledge workers didn't have a mobile device or a home office. Some didn't even have a personal computer. When they left work for the day or the weekend, or on leave or vacation, there was hardly any ability—much less an expectation—to remain available to their employers. Sure, they could get the odd phone call from work after hours, but work time was limited by very practical and tangible boundaries.

Today, most knowledge workers are attached to their jobs by the hip, literally. As it has gotten easier to accomplish minor or even major work tasks at home or on the go, there has been a growing expectation that workers remain available to answer the call (or email or Slack message) around the clock, especially in certain industries and roles. The circumstances that blur the boundaries between our work and home lives, however, can be used in entirely opposing ways. At Hailey's previous job, being reachable came with added pressures and expectations to put work ahead of life, both during and beyond working hours. In her current role, having the ability to answer a quick call from a client, or respond to a quick email when away from her desk has the opposite effect. Rather than making her feel like she can't escape work even when she's not physically at her desk, it allows her to detach from work more readily, knowing that she can still be reached if necessary.

Hailey says the mental separation she enjoys in her new job—knowing she's unlikely to be disturbed during her time off—has ironically led to some of her best work. That's especially the case since she adopted a mini goldendoodle named May during the pandemic. "I take her on long walks on Monday mornings, and I really try to not look at my phone during that time. And very often I will find my brain wandering to a pitch idea I know that I have on my to-do list and thinking of a really unique idea and then just jotting that down," she says, explaining that most of her best work ideas have struck during those absences from work.

Hailey's more relaxed lifestyle is quite typical of those who are given a four-day workweek. According to research from the UK pilot study, the most common use of the extra day off fell into the category "life admin," which included a wide range of personal errands, like grocery shopping, medical appointments, and household chores.[7] While some of these chores would typically fall to Saturday and Sundays, others, such as medical appointments, require leaving work in the middle of the day. For this reason, the four-day workweek can significantly reduce employee absenteeism. Furthermore, by taking care of these "life admin" tasks on a day that was previously designated for work, most study participants reported that they actually enjoyed time off during the weekend, the increased downtime ulti-mately helping them return to work more rested and energized.

The studies also show that a vast majority of those who switch to a four-day workweek are unwilling to switch back, and Hailey is one of them. Prior to joining Daly in 2020—before the company had piloted its Forever Summer Fridays and Slowdown Time schedule adjustments—she says she wasn't interested in working for any agency, instead preferring to remain in-house. "I thought I probably wouldn't be here for more than a few years," says Hailey, who was named one of *Business Insider*'s PR Rising Stars in 2023, an honor giving her the kind of profile that would make her a hot commodity on the job mar-ket. "Now, I truly don't think there is another company that I would want to work for."

Six months after making the switch to a thirty-two-hour schedule, Alex and Ally conducted an evaluation focused on the program's effects on employees and customers.

"Clients weren't writing to us that they weren't getting enough time or attention, team members were happy with how it was going, so we decided to formally make it part of our operations," says Ally.

Alex adds, "We also hear from so many of our client leads who do a lot of creative pitching and storytelling for their clients that they get their best ideas when they're not at the computer working. Maybe they go on a walk during their lunch break and, in the absence of staring at a screen, come up with a really great pitch angle for a client, or they get their best ideas in the shower or right when they're about to fall asleep, when they're not trying to think of something new. That's when those ideas have the space to come out, and I think that concept is true for creatives in general. You can't force it."

On the employee side, they reported lower stress levels, better time management, higher levels of motivation, and greater overall produc-tivity. "I'm now able to use Monday mornings to do things in my personal life that will set the stage for a more mindful and intentional workweek," wrote one employee on an anonymous feedback form. Another said, "The opportunity to slowly dive into the week makes it much less daunting, and starting work on Monday afternoon is something I now actively look forward to."

As for clients, Alex says both Daly's rate of reengagement with existing clients and the rate of new client contracts doubled during the six-month trial, faster than any other period in the company's history. "We learned that work will fill the space that you give it, and that can drive burnout," Alex and Ally wrote in a coauthored op-ed published by *Fast Company* in 2024. "If we can condense the workweek, we can still deliver excellent client services and maintain productivity but start giving time back to employees for their non-work life."[8]

Six months after making the switch, in early 2024, Daly made the reduced schedule permanent. "It's in our handbook and operations manual, and now it's a permanent part of Daly's benefits and offering," Ally tells us. "At the end of each year, we reevaluate what's working and what's not," Alex adds. "I don't see a world in which this is not one of our core offerings, but I could see it changing—maybe we cut back further on hours."

11 A Recruitment and Retention Game Changer

There was no way for Jay Goldman to win the tech recruiting arms race against global superpowers.

The cofounder and CEO of Toronto-based enterprise software platform Sensei Labs says that half of his fifty-five-person team is made up of software engineers, and in 2021, the company was losing talent. It was just over a year after his firm had spun out of Klick Health—a marketing agency and commercialization partner for life sciences products—and competition for engineering talent was fierce. Just as the company was getting off the ground, tech industry giants were approaching his candidates and staff with salary offers the company simply couldn't match. "We had lost a few developers who very much did not want to go, but who were made offers that they really just couldn't say no to," Jay explains. "They would come to us and say, 'I really don't want to do this. What should I do?' And we would just say to them, 'We can't match that kind of salary increase. This is meaningful for you and your family, so go and take it.'"[1]

It was around that time that Jay found himself attending a talk by Juliet Schor, one of Joe's research collaborators, who mentioned recruitment and retention as a key benefit of the shorter workweek. That observation got Jay thinking. "We have always tried to follow a path when it comes to competition of any kind—competition for talent included—where we think, 'How do we change the game to something that they can't or won't play?'" he says. "There's no way for us to match the kinds of salaries that were coming out of the Amazons and Facebooks of the world at the time, so if we can't beat them at their game, how do we change to a different game they won't be able to play?" A few months later, Sensei Labs signed up to participate in Joe's second four-day workweek trial in the United States.

Before making the switch, however, Jay made it clear to his staff that the experiment was only that. While he kept the door open to maintaining the policy indefinitely, he was careful to communicate how it could only continue past the initial trial phase if it passed a rigorous evaluation six months later. "One of the most useful exercises that came out of this—and I think something that you could only do as a leader when you're offering an incentive to the team—was to really pressurize all of our systems into finding those productivity leaks and gaps that we weren't even really aware of," Jay explains. "If you go to your team and say, 'Everybody be 20 percent more productive,' everyone's just going to be like, 'Yeah, whatever. I'm busy.' But if you go to them and say, 'You can have Fridays off if you find ways to be 20 percent more productive,' you get a lot of really great suggestions about how you could be 20 percent more productive, or more."

Jay adds that those productivity gains came in many of the usual ways that trial participants cut down on wasted time. For instance, the team members eliminated unnecessary meetings and reduced the length and number of participants for the necessary ones. The new approach also enabled certain processes that had previously required synchronized collaboration to become asynchronous, which allowed staff to work continuously, with fewer bottlenecks (more on that in chapter 14). Sensei Labs also asked the staff to move all of their personal appointments to their new day off rather than eating up work time. This clearing up of schedules ultimately gave staff more uninterrupted focus time in the thirty-two-hour workweek than was typically enjoyed with the forty-hour one.

"We had every team do an exercise of thinking through how to benchmark productivity for themselves," Jay adds. "Some of the teams came back with sort of vanity metrics, and we had to explain to them why it wasn't a valid metric and push back on it. It was a useful exercise because it made me realize that most people don't have a good sense of how the company makes money and how its economics operate, and so when you ask them to think about something like productivity, they don't really understand how productivity connects back to the business itself." On learning that many of his teams were prioritizing tasks and metrics that didn't move the needle on business outcomes, Jay worked with them to better focus their efforts on the things that really contribute to the bottom line. "We sometimes refer to this as 'outcomes versus optics,'" he explains. "The optics of being productive are quite easy to game in most organizations, once you figure out what the optics are, but it doesn't mean you're being more productive." (No, Jay did not get an advance copy of chapter 5 on redefining productivity, nor was he coerced or deceived into providing a response that so perfectly aligned with our thinking on the subject.)

As Jay expected, the first few weeks of the trial presented some unexpected challenges. For example, Sensei Labs initially let teams decide for themselves whether to take either Mondays or Fridays off, but Jay soon realized that the organization had suddenly gone from five days of cross-team collaboration to just three. After seeing how such a sudden and drastic change created new and unnecessary challenges, Jay's cofounder Benji Nadler moved everyone to a Monday-to-Thursday schedule. Then, to avoid any customer catastrophes on Fridays, Sensei Labs asked each customer-facing team to designate one member to be on call that day on a rotating schedule. "Our customer teams have one person that checks-in three times a day—9 a.m., noon, and 3 p.m.—and handles any escalations that come up, but generally they're able to just push things off until the Monday or just open a support ticket," Jay says. "For our engineering teams on call, for them, that only means they can't be more than ten minutes from a keyboard. They can do whatever they want with their day off, but they have to be able to log on within ten minutes, just in case. Not the whole team, just whoever's on call that day."

———————

In the more than two years since the initial six-month pilot began in 2022 Sensei Labs has had four formal reviews of the policy, and Jay says each one has only further reinforced its effectiveness.

Despite the ongoing success, however, Jay says he doesn't intend to drop the semiannual checkup anytime soon. "We have maintained the right with our team to cancel this if it doesn't continue to work, and I think that cadence of discipline has been really helpful in keeping people focused on productivity, instead of falling back into old ways and maybe letting that productivity slip," he explains, adding that the four-day workweek continues to be a source of motivation more than two years later. "The impact on our team has been so significant; I've had so many conversations with team members who have told me how life-changing it's been for them," he adds.

Jay explains that the company still offers competitive salaries in line with local industry standards and employee expectations but uses the shorter schedule to compete against foreign industry giants with significantly higher staffing budgets. In terms of its monetary value, Jay originally thought of the four-day workweek as equivalent to a 20 percent salary boost, suggesting that he can remain competitive with any employer offering up to 20 percent more—which, as explained earlier, is a conservative estimate. As described in chapter 6, some 33 percent of trial participants in the North American pilot program conducted by 4 Day Week Global said they would demand a salary increase of between 26 and 50 percent to switch back to a five-day schedule, 12 percent would demand more than 50 percent more money, and 14 percent said no amount of money would persuade them to return to a five-day rotation. "What we've now heard from our team, which is consistent with what the research in the field has found, is that it's probably more like a 30 percent increase," he says.

Ironically, Jay piloted the four-day workweek in 2022 out of fear of losing the half of his team that was composed of engineering talent. In the more than two years since, however, the tech industry has contracted, and engineering talent has become less scarce. Now it is the other half of the organization that he says would be considered a flight risk, as the market for customer success and solution engineering jobs grows more competitive. "I don't know that I could put a direct dollar amount on a productivity value to the business, but I would say that the impact to our culture and to our team—the retention value, the talent attraction value—has been incredible," Jay says, adding that he will continue to win as long as others refuse to play the game. "I really hope that nobody else adopts this," he adds, half-jokingly, "because it's been a really big competitive advantage for us."

Recruitment and retention were also a primary motivator behind Grand Challenges Canada's switch to a shorter schedule, according to Tracy Smith, senior director of people and culture.[2]

Tracy says that, like the staff of many nonprofits, her 115 team members tend to be young, passionate, and enthusiastic, often sacrificing personal enrichment for the opportunity to make a positive difference in the world. It is those same motivations, however, that can result in high turnover. Those who are so passionate about a cause that they'll dedicate their careers to it aren't always prone to taking days off, and while that commitment is admirable, it's often not sustainable. "Our work can be taxing on individuals; we are dealing with heavy topics," she says. Couple an emotionally taxing day job with highly passionate individuals who won't rest until the job is done, and you've got a recipe for potential turnover.

Tracy says the Covid-19 pandemic also had an impact on applicant priorities. "The pandemic was such a game changer," she says. "A lot of people reprioritized and realized what their nonnegotiables were, and flexibility is one of those things. People have come to value the present day, among all generations, but especially younger folks. It's about living their best life today, not waiting until retirement."

That is ultimately what inspired Grand Challenges Canada to champion a four-day workweek trial, which—like Sensei Labs—the organization began in the fall of 2022. Over the six months that followed, staff were given Fridays off from work. Six months later, Grand Challenges Canada conducted an evaluation of the program, with the emphasis split between outcomes for internal staff and external stakeholders. "Overwhelmingly there was support, both internally and externally, for the program," Tracy says. "The only change that we made was that in the beginning, we suggested that Fridays were more like holidays, but we now call them 'Flex Fridays' and we ask people to be reachable, because we do recognize that we are still an organization that serves others and that there are still things that could come up on a Friday. If an employee really wants to be unreachable, we ask them to book a vacation day. Otherwise, once a quarter, they might get a text because someone needs something on a Friday. But we had to make that clarification."

Tracy says that since that initial adjustment to the trial program in early 2023, the four-day workweek has otherwise remained unchanged. "As far as I can see, it's continued to be highly successful in all aspects," she says. "The four-day workweek is both a reward and a retention strategy, given that this type of work can be really tough, and it can be hard to take vacation when you feel that sense of commitment and passion. We are literally trying to institutionalize time off, because they are tremendously hard workers."

———————

For much of the last century, employers called the shots. In just the last couple of decades, the balance of power has shifted in the opposite direction, where it's likely to remain for the foreseeable future, even if the pendulum briefly swings in the opposite direction on occasion, as seen in the years immediately following the Great Resignation.

The labor market operates just like any other; when inventory is high, prices go down, and when inventory is low, prices go up. Over the last two hundred years or so, starting with the industrial revolution, workers have typically outnumbered jobs, meaning that buyers—or in this case, employers—often got to dictate terms. In recent years, however, data suggests that the equation has flipped, with more open positions than available workers across most industries and skill categories.

Every major economic shock causes a spike in the unemployment rate, but if you read between the outliers, a clear pattern emerges. Take out spikes in unemployment caused by the 2020 pandemic, the 2008 recession, and the 2001 dot-com crash, and you'll find an unemployment rate that's been in steady decline for much of the twenty-first century.[3] During most of the 1970s, 1980s, and 1990s, US unemployment hovered between 5 and 10 percent, but in 2000, it dipped below 4 percent for the first time since the start of the Nixon administration, in 1969.[4] Unemployment shot back up during the dot-com crash of 2001, settled back down to 4.4 percent in 2006, shot back up during the 2008 recession, and then fell all the way down to 3.5 percent by 2019.[5] After another spike during the pandemic, it settled back down to that near-record low of 3.5 percent in 2022. Although the rate keeps seesawing, it continues to drop lower with each turn, and there's reason to believe the dips will only get lower in the coming years.

The latest fall in unemployment was particularly challenging for businesses. A white-hot economy, rising costs, and pent-up postpandemic career restlessness led to the now-infamous Great Resignation. In 2021, a record-breaking 47.8 million Americans walked off the job.[6] To put that number in perspective, most years see about 30 million resignations. In weak economies, like that of 2009, they fall to the low-20 millions, and in strong economies, like that of 2006 or 2016, they push closer to 35 million. The record set by 2021 didn't last long, however, as resignations topped 50.5 million the following year.[7]

During that time, companies like Healthwise—a nonprofit based in Boise, Idaho, that develops educational content for the health-care sector—saw its annual attrition rate jump from about 10 percent to 18 percent. That means the company had to replace nearly one in five of its workers during those years. To stop the bleeding, CEO Adam Husney consulted with Joe to implement a four-day workweek. "Our attrition rate went from 18 percent to several quarters of 0 percent and stabilized at about 2 percent," he says. "Staff satisfaction was very high, with over 90 percent of employees rating the company a four or five out of five. We were much more easily able to hire for open positions. This allowed us to be much more selective in our hiring."[8]

When the municipal employees of San Juan County in Washington State demanded a nearly $1 million pay raise that the local government couldn't afford in 2023, the county instead reduced its workweek to four days without any changes in compensation.[9] In the year that followed, the county saw an 85 percent increase in job applications, a 43 percent decline in turnover, and a 23 percent reduction in sick days.

Though the Great Resignation is behind us, it probably won't be the last major shock to the supply side of the labor market. As discussed earlier in the book, US population growth is in decline, along with most other Western nations. The Bureau of Labor Statistics also anticipates that labor market participation rates will continue to decline over the next decade as baby boomers retire out of the workforce and aren't replaced by as many young people. By 2030, every member of the largest generation in American history—which numbers around 73 million, over a fifth of the country—will be over the age of sixty-five, in what has been dubbed the *silver tsunami*.[10] Perhaps it's unsurprising then that the Bureau of Labor Statistics predicts that health-care support will be the fastest growing job sector over the next decade, as more workers are needed to care for an aging population. That industry is expected to grow by 15.2 percent over the next ten years, more than any other in the economy, while health-care practitioners placed third, with an expected growth of 8.6 percent.

The second-largest area of employment growth, according to the bureau, is "computer and mathematics"—in other words, tech. The rise in this area also makes sense, given the growth of both the technology industry and the increasing demand for tech skills in just about every other sector. In fact, 2024 was the first year in which non-tech-industry employers hired more tech talent than the industry itself, according to global real estate services company CBRE.[11] That means that most major organizations, within and far beyond the tech industry, are facing a problem similar to the one Jay Goldman faced in 2021. They are competing for the same talent as some of the world's largest and wealthiest employers.

Between the aging population, the shrinking pool of talent, and the rapidly shifting needs of a technology industry that is more embedded in more industries every day, employers need to recognize that they are no longer dictating the terms of employment agreements, at least not when it comes to certain high-value skills. As we saw during the Great Resignation, employees are more willing to quit their jobs today than in generations past, largely because there are more opportunities available to them if they do. In 2022, the average tenure for workers aged eighteen to thirty-four was just 2.8 years.[12] And there is a growing body of research that suggests young people can advance their careers and increase their earnings faster by switching jobs, not staying in them.[13] According to a 2025 survey of thirty-eight thousand working adults across thirty-four countries by human capital management services and software provider ADP, 75 percent leave before getting promoted.

That's an expensive prospect for their employers. Even the most conservative estimates suggest the cost of replacing one staff member is between one-half and two times their annual salary. In 2019—before the pandemic and the Great Resignation—turnover cost the US economy over $1 trillion, according to Gallup, and there's reason to believe the problem will only get worse.[14] As employers compete to attract the next generation of workers—the generation that prizes personal time and flexibility over compensation, switches jobs more readily in pursuit of promotions and better work-life balance, strives to work for organizations that share their values—the four-day workweek will become an even more appealing prospect.

We are not suggesting that every company should implement a four-day workweek to attract employees. In fact, if every company did so, that would effectively cancel out the competitive advantages this approach offers as a recruitment tool. But we are saying that organizations that can't compete for workers by outspending the competition can use it to their advantage. In other words, if you, like Jay Goldman, are financially outmatched by the competition, the only way to win is to change the game. You don't need to offer top dollar *and* a shorter workweek *and* generous access to remote and hybrid work. But if you want to compete in an increasingly tight market for talent, you probably need to offer at least one.

12 But What about My Clients?

When a digital marketing campaign goes live, the ads start working around the clock, and often that means the people managing them behind the scenes are too.

Though they don't require constant supervision, the brands running those campaigns could reach out to their agency partner at any moment during a campaign to request immediate changes to pricing information, visuals, messaging, strategy, or other elements. "Marketing is kind of a twenty-four-seven thing," explains Chris Leone, the CEO of Geear (which rebranded from WebStrategies, Inc., in 2025), a digital marketing agency based in Richmond, Virginia, that primarily works with credit unions. "Things happen at all times of the day, and so we have to be prepared for that and stay ready to respond."[1]

When Chris first heard about the four-day workweek sometime in mid-2021, he admits that he—like many business owners on first learning of the concept—scoffed at the idea: "There was an employee survey about what we could do to make things better, and someone said, 'A four-day workweek,' and I laughed at it." Chris's thinking, however, began to change in 2022, when the company started facing the widespread employee attraction and retention challenges that came with the postpandemic Great Resignation—the same difficulties Jay Goldman of Sensei Labs described in the previous chapter.

From its founding in 2004, the forty-five-person company has managed to stay ahead of the industry's highly competitive talent marketplace by offering a fully remote work environment. By 2022, however, working from home was no longer a competitive differentiator. "Staffing and retaining great people and hiring great people was harder in 2022 than it had been in a very long time, and that was enough to get us thinking about what we can do to make this a more competitive place for people to work," Chris explains. "As a small company, we just can't pay these insane salaries."

As time went on and as he kept reading more about Joe's four-day pilots in major business publications, Chris decided to engage in something of a thought experiment. Instead of dismissing the idea, he let himself disregard his biggest hesitation and accepted the possibility that his staff could be as productive in four days as they currently were in five. "After I let myself get over that mental hurdle, I thought of all the other stuff that would happen," he says. "It would make it such a great place to work, we'd be able to give back to our people; we'd be able to do more for our mission."

Chris says what really pushed him over the edge, however, was considering how different the company's future would be if it hired and retained the industry's best and brightest. "I only needed 20 percent [more productivity] to make up for the Fridays off, and an A player can be three, four, five, ten times more efficient—I can make that up in a heartbeat," he says. "And if the incentive is, you get an extra day on your weekend if you can figure out how to get stuff done faster, people are going to shorten their meetings, they're not going to extend stuff, they're not taking [unnecessarily] long breaks during the day; they're going to get it done because they want that outcome."

Convincing himself of the feasibility of a four-day workweek, however, was only the first step. Once he decided that he was willing to give it a try, Chris had to confront the challenge of managing client expectations in an industry that requires a particularly high degree of timely communications. The many changes that he implemented in the run-up to Geear's four-day trial—which began with a month of half day Fridays in June 2023—included giving staff permission to decline or shorten meetings and challenging them to cut turnaround times by 20 percent. The following month, when the four-day trial began in earnest, he asked employees to check their inboxes three times each Friday to ensure they hadn't missed any timely client requests.

Chris then developed a communication decision tree that guides staff when messages land in their inbox on their new day off. "We said, 'Under these circumstances, you have to involve other team members in an initiative on a Friday,'" he says, adding that employees are expected to take a vacation day if they truly won't be reachable on a Friday. "So if a client's like, 'Hey, our rates just changed on a loan product, and we're running ads that advertise the wrong rate,' we're going to jump on that. If a client's like, 'Hey, I need to cut my budget this month. Can you please turn this ad off so we don't spend more?' we will do that day-of," Chris continues. "But if a client comes to us and they're like, 'Hey, we want to go into a new market and want to know how much it would cost; can you let me know?' according to the decision tree, that waits until next week."

On further reflection, Chris admits that some version of the decision tree already existed, albeit informally, for timely requests that landed in staff inboxes outside of standard working hours. Like many industries today, digital marketing is rarely confined to typical business hours. Though his staff members now sometimes need to take a few hours on the occasional Friday to respond to time-sensitive client needs, Chris says it's still a dramatic improvement from industry norms. "In the marketing world, where we're notorious for sixty-hour workweeks, that's still not bad," he says. In fact, Chris says even though some team members occasionally need to work for a few hours on some Fridays, those days are often spent on tasks that would have previously bled into their weekends. "People who do put in some time on a Friday, it's kind of like clearing the desk work," he says. "It's like, 'I had a lot of meetings, I need to organize some notes, I want to just clear the plate, clear the inbox, get everything sorted, and then by 10:30, I'm done and I have the rest of my day.' And they like having time where no meetings are booked and nobody is hitting them up on Slack."

Chris, who says he often takes a scientific approach to business decisions, conducted something of a blind test with Geear's customers and opted not to inform them of the change. Six months later, he measured the results of the pilot against a range of metrics, each of which he told his staff would determine whether the program would continue. "We had to keep hitting our financial and customer satisfaction metrics—those were nonnegotiables," he says.

As the experiment continued, Chris says some of the benefits he had expected did ultimately materialize, along with others he hadn't anticipated. "One of the most notable findings was that we saw about a 20 percent decrease in the time that it took to complete tasks," he says, adding that the data was readily available in the company's internal task management software. "So it played out as we hoped; people were finding ways to do things in less time." Equally important to Chris, however, was the effect on the employee net promoter score, or eNPS, which anonymously asks staff members how likely they are to recommend Geear as an employer to others. For the five quarters before Geear adopted a four-day workweek, the company's eNPS score averaged 52. In the five quarters since, it has averaged 82. "It helped keep great people around, it helped our ability to attract great people to work here, which in turn allows us to do better work for our clients," he says.

One year after the experiment began, Chris reports that the company has grown 22 percent despite an otherwise challenging period for the industry, during which time most companies saw revenues drop or remain flat. "Our retention rate of clients is about as good as it gets in our industry; the average is about 18 percent annual churn, and we have around 8 percent," he says. "We've been able to grow as a company, we've improved our financial metrics, the eNPS is up, and we've had a great growth year." Though he once laughed at the thought of moving the company to a four-day schedule, Chris says he has no plans to switch back. "As long as we continue to execute on our KPIs [key performance indicators], I see no reason to stop."

There are some undeniable challenges associated with being a four-day company in a five-day world.

An individual organization might see the merits of work time reduction, but what about its clients? Its contractors? Its suppliers? How will the market perceive its commitment against its competitors? Often, getting ahead means doing things differently, but doing things differently means being out of sync with those who maintain the status quo, at least temporarily. That is perhaps why, when we talk to folks about the four-day workweek, the most common response we hear is something along the lines of, "It sounds good in theory, but I have clients/customers/suppliers/other stakeholders that depend on my business five days a week, so it just won't work for us." On mentioning our work in this field, we often see this mental journey playing out in real time: first a glimmer of hope—and even glee—at the thought of getting a day back each week, then the faint smile fades as the "business brain" takes over and reminds them of their five-day responsibilities. This hurdle, however, often looms larger in the mind than in reality, and in the previous pages, we've met many leaders that have found creative solutions, including some who shared those initial hesitations. Despite some expected short-term hiccups, all these leaders have found a way to operate on a four-day schedule without negatively impacting their external stakeholders. In fact, most report that their clients are intrigued, even impressed, rather than hostile.

Throughout the previous chapters, we have offered examples of organizations that took their own approach to adopting a four-day schedule in a way that enabled them to maintain or even surpass their earlier performance. For example, Unilever New Zealand and Unilever Australia let staff build their own four-day schedules and trusted them to choose their day off in light of individual job requirements. "No two people are the same, no two weeks are the same, and no two jobs are the same in terms of what they require from people," explains managing director Cameron Heath. The staggered schedule means that most teams have at least one member on staff during standard operating hours, but employees are still expected to make themselves available on the fifth day when necessary.

Simon Ursell says that his organization, Tyler Grange, became more responsive to clients after eliminating Fridays, because of the technological overhaul that accompanied the change in schedule. The change, he says, would have been impossible without the incentive of a shorter workweek.

Leena Yousefi of YLaw told us that the firm still maintains at least one support staff member across all five days, and that it's not uncommon for her lawyers to put in an extra hour or two on the day off, a practice she says is still in keeping with the spirit of the policy.

Alex Daly and Ally Bruschi specifically designed their agency's thirty-two-hour weekly schedule in a way that provides coverage for all five days, while only removing the hours that clients are least likely to call with emergency needs—namely, Monday mornings, Friday afternoons, and the last half hour of the day on Tuesdays, Wednesdays, and Thursdays.

After a brief trial period, Tracy Smith of Grand Challenges Canada amended the four-day workweek policy to specify that the extra day was not a holiday but rather a flex day and that staff were still accountable to external stakeholders on those days. "If an employee really wants to be unreachable, we ask them to book a vacation day," she says.

Jay Goldman told us about how Sensei Labs designates a staff member from each team to be on call during the fifth day on a rotating schedule. When their week comes up, the designated customer team member has to check in three times a day, and the designated member of the engineering team needs to remain within ten minutes of a keyboard.

Each company we've met thus far has demonstrated how organizations often find creative solutions for managing the one-day gap in a way that best suits their unique needs. Each also expressed how managing client expectations during the fifth day caused a lot more anxiety than necessary, as the problem ultimately proved much less significant than they had anticipated.

Throughout this book, we've also explored how, unlike in past generations, work in the digital age is no longer truly confined to designated workdays. Even in a standard nine-to-five, Monday-to-Friday rotation, workers are typically reachable around the clock. It's not uncommon for employees today to answer an email or put in some important or timely work from home during evenings and weekends, especially in certain industries, roles, or levels of seniority. That is why, when people express concerns about not being available to clients and external stakeholders all five days, we usually respond by asking them what they do when a client or stakeholder needs their attention on evenings and weekends. Typically, they'll tell us about how they respond to emails on their phone, or make a quick call, or rush to a computer to do some touch-ups on client work, and so on—some even do so on vacation. These days, many people also have automated self-service tools that customers can use to independently manage more-basic needs during nonoperating hours. Whatever response they provide usually applies to how they would and should handle a client's needs on the fifth day after switching to a four-day workweek.

For organizations with particularly demanding clients or that are likely to receive an emergency request on that fifth day, Joe often recommends the Sensei Labs approach: that is, designating a single member of each team to be on call during the fifth day. That, he says, not only ensures proactive coverage but also lets the rest of the team breathe a little easier on their days off. Just as we'd all probably prefer to have someone covering our desks while we're on vacation, designating that person helps us fully detach from work and avoid returning to a pile of pending requests.

––––––––––––

Though the firm's project portfolio was growing rapidly in 2022, SMA Architecture + Design's profits were not growing with it.

As the forty-person commercial architecture and design firm took on more clients, staff were putting in longer hours, but all the extra effort had failed to make a meaningful impact on the organization's bottom line. "For at least a year and a half, the conversation in the firm between us and with all of our staff was always, 'We've got to get more efficient,'" explains the company's principal and partner Jason Davis from the company's head office in Helena, Montana, nestled between the Rocky Mountains to the west and the Great Plains to the east.[2] "We were creating a lot of new systems within the firm, like checklists for different phases of projects, so when you're in the schematic design phase, here's the checklist, these are the things that you should and shouldn't be doing." During this period, Jason says, his colleague and fellow partner Klint Fisher spent months developing new tools, systems, and resources to help move the needle on productivity. "We kept trying different things, and eventually I started to think, 'Do we need to introduce something really big into the firm to try to effect some change?'"

It was around that time that Jason started reading about Joe's four-day workweek trials. At first he dismissed the idea, afraid that the other partners would laugh him out of the room if he suggested addressing their productivity problems by cutting back on work hours. Over time, however, as the company exhausted more options, the leadership team began to express interest in trying something bold. "I was still nervous," Jason says. "I thought about it for probably three or four months before I finally got up the nerve to walk into one of our weekly principals meetings and say 'Hey, I've got a wild idea here,' and I kind of pitched it to the other principals." He adds that their reaction was not at all what he had expected. "They all pretty quickly went, 'Huh, that's really interesting.' Tim, my business partner, was like, 'That's exactly what we need, something big like that,' so the principal group embraced it quicker, easier than I thought, and I wished I had brought it up a few months prior to that." In hindsight, Jason says giving his staff all the tools, processes, and training in the world was of little use without a real incentive for adopting them.

SMA, however, was hesitant to eliminate one full day from the workweek at first, largely out of fear of jeopardizing certain key external relationships. "We have clients that expect us to be available when they need us; we have contractors that expect us to be available when they need us while they're on construction projects. And then we have consultants as well," Jason explains. "We're the head of the projects, and we have engineers that work for us that we hire, and they need us when they need us."

Ironically, when Jason presented the idea of eliminating Fridays, it was his most productive staff who expressed the kind of hesitation he had originally anticipated from his fellow partners. "'We're already working more than forty hours. How are we going to do this in less time?'" Jason recalls them saying.

"They felt like they were doing a lot of work," adds principal and studio director Mark Ophus. "There was so much more work to do, and we weren't pulling in a profit—it was hard to give bonuses and raises." Before committing to a four-day pilot, Mark says, he had to assure the team that the policy was optional and that those who were struggling to make deadlines wouldn't be forced to take time off if doing so only added to their stress. "People are going to find a way to make it work for them," he says. "And if people are stressed—and we have a lot of people who are just natural stressors—we aren't forcing them to take the day off. We spent a lot of time discussing the terminology, and we frame it as being a gift that's flexible. We still have a contract that is five days a week, so it becomes a carrot to get that fifth day off."

The second element that Jason and Mark had to provide to truly give their staff extra time off from work was some sort of guarantee that their clients and stakeholders wouldn't be left waiting for them to return to their desks. Jason explains that, thanks to industry norms and standards, staff already felt uncomfortable letting client calls go to voicemail, even on evenings and weekends. "We have coached some of our people to just not take that call. Like, you've got to retrain that client a little bit: 'You're a person, you have a real life, you're not always available.' And there's very few—*very few*—instances in our world of architecture that are true emergencies and can't wait a day," he says. SMA also made a habit of reaching out to its clients later in the week to check in and make sure there weren't any pending needs that could arise during their time off that they should be aware of. "We communicate out to them so they're not necessarily looking for us, and the same with contractors," Jason says.

Mark adds, "The benefit of maybe not being available on the Friday is they usually solve the problem themselves before Monday anyway. If a client is needing something for real, we take care of it. That's something everybody in the leadership group—and we've got maybe ten people in that right now—we all kind of committed to doing that for staff."

Mark, a self-described workaholic, says he prefers to spend his Fridays enjoying the quieter pace of the otherwise-empty office to do the heads-down work he rarely has time for during the rest of the week—work he used to do on his actual weekends. "I'm using it specifically for certain things," he explains. "It just keeps me more focused on stuff I'm not actually able to get to during the rest of the busy week because we have clients calling or people who need help on production or a code problem or something else, and it's just quieter." Jason, however, prefers to enjoy his days off outside of the office, though he, like the rest of the leadership team, commits to keeping an eye on his email so that the rest of the staff can detach from work worry-free. "It gives us the opportunity to do something more for people," he says. "As leaders, we're kind of sacrificing ourselves a little bit to make this work."

In October 2023, the company piloted a three-month-long half-day Friday program and, in January 2024, progressed to a four-day workweek pilot. "Most of our clients didn't know that we had started to take Fridays off," Jason says. He adds that SMA has been able to hire some of the best and brightest in the region, after years of struggling to compete for talent in a relatively limited pool. Mark adds, "It's something we could promote to try and hire better people to just elevate the firm, make it a better place to work, do better projects, do projects better, that sort of thing."

After conducting a review and consulting with staff in late 2024, six months after moving to a four-day workweek, SMA decided to revert to a flexible four-and-a-half-day policy, with the intention of returning to a four-day workweek in the near future. Through the process, Mark says SMA has learned a lot about the firm, explaining that the experiment has acted as "a catalyst for change to improve the health of our company." SMA's journey illustrates that while not every organization will be ready for a full four-day workweek, the process of examination and experimentation can deliver genuine progress for employee well-being and balance. It also demonstrates how, by positioning it as a trial, a pilot, or an experiment, organizations can tweak and adjust the policy over time to suit their unique needs. Even if a four-day workweek isn't the best option right now, simply engaging in the process can help you find organizational efficiencies, energize your staff, and establish a longer-term goal to work toward collectively.

The deeper benefit of SMA's four-day workweek pilot, however, was put into sharp focus just a couple of months after the start of the trial, when Klint—one of the partners responsible for championing the effort—passed away just eight months after being diagnosed with pancreatic cancer. He was forty-nine years old when he died on February 24, 2024. "Klint's passing has certainly taught me over this last year that there are so many more important things in life outside of the office," Jason says, adding that it demonstrated how this most precious commodity, time, is so easily taken for granted. "If we as business owners can give our staff the gift of more time away from the office with their families, to me personally, I think that is worth more than any amount of money I could pay somebody to be here." If Klint were still around today, Jason says, he'd probably be spending his Fridays fly fishing, which he did almost every day he had off from work. "He was a dear friend," adds Mark. "We all miss him a lot."

PART THREE

_____

The Four-Day Blueprint

How to Do More in Four

13 Advocating for a Four-Day Workweek

Throughout this book, we've demonstrated why it's time for a shorter workweek, and we've introduced some of the internal advocates who have made it a reality at their organization. Now, we're asking you to join them.

As we discussed in the opening pages, changes to the workweek are rarely brought about by political mandate, at least not before a certain degree of organic critical mass. Instead, most of the biggest changes to how we've worked in the past have been driven by well-organized employees and forward-thinking business leaders, and this revolution is no different. As an early advocate on this topic and as the CEO of Work Time Revolution and the former CEO of 4 Day Week Global, Joe has spent the last eight years in the trenches working with these internal champions, helping them take the idea from concept to reality. In his experience, the transformation often starts with one person. If you've made it this far in the book, we're hoping that's you.

While the process is certainly streamlined when that internal cheerleader is the ultimate decision-maker—like the CEO of a small company without influential investors or board members—even they need to get their teams on board for the necessary changes to make it a success. One person can make the four-day workweek a reality—we've seen them do so successfully countless times—but not if they act alone.

In our experience, implementing a four-day workweek often requires a certain degree of research, collaboration, and patience. Asking your manager or boss to let staff work one day less while still enjoying the same level of compensation will probably be a tough sell. As with Henry Ford's decision to implement a forty-hour week, your leaders will respond better to an appeal anchored in performance and productivity. For any strong argument, you'll have to consider the other person's perspective and base your case on the three tenets of persuasion: ethos (credibility), pathos (emotion), and logos (logic and reason). Through his experience working with hundreds of internal champions and business leaders on their four-day journeys, Joe has come up with a six-step formula for explaining the merits of a shorter workweek to employers in terms that are often most appealing to them.

Step 1: Consider Their Perspective

If you're going to win over your boss, you'll need to put the four-day workweek in terms that speak to them. In Joe's experience, there are three primary motivations that drive an organization to adopt a four-day workweek. Identifying which will appeal the most to your employer is the first step in crafting a proposal that can grab their attention.

The first incentive is the opportunity to differentiate their employee value proposition and stand out from the crowd as an employer. As we explored earlier, organizations of all shapes and sizes can benefit from the attraction and retention boost that comes from adopting a four-day workweek. This appeal, however, is especially effective when made to leaders struggling to compete for highly competitive skills—either because they operate in an industry or a market where specialized talent is scarce or because they're up against larger and better-funded competitors, or both.

Second is the chance to improve employee well-being and reduce burnout, which can have greater appeal to leaders who operate in high-pressure industries or work environments. As exemplified by Leena Yousefi of YLaw, this is a particularly effective approach for addressing business leaders who have experienced burnout firsthand; unfortunately, this group includes more leaders than not. A 2023 *Harvard Business Review* study, for example, found that 53 percent of managers feel burned-out on most days.[1] Family law also epitomizes an industry with particularly high burnout rates and, with it, notably high sick leave, absenteeism, and turnover costs for employers, but there are plenty more examples of similar challenges in very different organizations. Employee well-being was also a key motivating factor for Tracy Smith of Grand Challenges Canada, a nonprofit that operates in an emotionally taxing sector. Over the years, Joe has worked with business leaders in law, the nonprofit sector, finance, media, advertising, manufacturing, and other fields that struggle with absenteeism because of the nature of the work or the competitiveness of the industry. If your employer is looking for a way to address the burnout problem or simply to improve employee morale in a way that encourages greater engagement, the four-day workweek has proven effective.

Third, many organizations switch to a four-day workweek to improve productivity. That is especially true among organizations that have tried and failed to implement significant technological adoption, like AI implementation, or other organizational changes aimed at increasing productivity.

Improving productivity was a key motivating factor for Chris Leone at Geear, the partners of SMA Architecture + Design, Cameron Heath of Unilever New Zealand, and Simon Ursell of Tyler Grange, all of whom shared their stories in earlier chapters. Each of these leaders described how they had long tried to implement big organizational improvements with limited success until they used the four-day workweek as an incentive. Instead of asking their people to put in the extra work to adopt new processes or technologies for the benefit of the business, they secured enthusiastic buy-in by letting their staff share in those gains through a shorter workweek. In chapter 4, we also outlined how the need to adopt new tools and processes will only become more pronounced in the quickly approaching age of AI. We shared some studies that showed how organizations that adopt the four-day work-week are more successful in those implementation efforts.

While these are the three primary motivators—attraction and retention, well-being and burnout, and productivity improvement initiatives—there are many other benefits to share with your orga-nization's key decision makers as well. As discussed in chapter 7, the four-day workweek also offers measurable sustainability benefits that can help organizations achieve their ESG goals and advance their corporate values. The four-day workweek has also proven especially beneficial for working parents and offers an effective way to address workforce gender gaps.

Some leaders also pride themselves on being forward-thinking, innovative, and bold and are naturally driven by the opportunity to be an early adopter of a new trend. As Jared can attest to from his reporting, the leaders who adopt the four-day workweek at this rel-atively early stage tend to get a lot of media attention, extra time on keynote stages, and good buzz among their industry peers. For many leaders, the public relations benefits of being an early adopter is a key motivator for being a first mover, and that particular benefit will expire sooner than later.

As you consider how to best pitch the four-day workweek, take some time to think about the kind of decision makers you're appealing to and which of these key benefits are most likely to resonate with them.

Step 2: Do Your Research

Now that you've taken some time to empathize with your manager or employer (pathos), it's time to start building a fact-based argument for considering a four-day workweek (logos) to solve some of their key business challenges. Using the latest research will help establish your credibility (ethos).

As we've explored throughout this book and as Joe has seen countless times in the real world, the four-day workweek is often initially met with skepticism, even among eventual adopters and evangelists. While we all know the merits by now (assuming you didn't just skip ahead to this chapter), it's important not to lose sight of how the idea of reducing work time while improving outcomes is entirely counterintuitive. The best way to combat the inevitable skepticism is to come prepared with data, research, and case studies to demonstrate the paradoxical reality of the initiative. Fortunately, there is a lot of data out there to help quell their reasonable skepticism, and more by the day. Assuming you can't just get your manager, employer, or key decision makers to read this whole book (we get it, it's long), here are a few key metrics that can help create an opening to a broader conversation. As you consider which data to include in your appeal, it's important to tie the information back to some of the key motivators you identified in step 1.

As described in chapter 3, in the original North American pilot program led by Joe, the forty-one employers that participated saw an average revenue increase of 15 percent over the twelve-month term, and employees ranked the experience a 9.1 out of 10. If your employer is spending significant time, energy, and resources addressing employee attraction and retention issues or struggling to compete for talent in a highly competitive field, consider sharing some of the data around just how much employees would be willing to sacrifice to maintain the policy after the pilot ended. When researchers asked what it would take for them to willingly switch back to a five-day schedule at the end of the pilot, 45 percent said they would demand a salary increase of at least 26 percent, and another 14 percent said no amount of money would persuade them to return to a five-day rotation.

If your employer, however, is more likely to be persuaded by the opportunity to implement significant organizational efficiencies with enthusiastic employee buy-in, refer to some of the data we shared in chapter 4. There we explored how an estimated 80 percent of AI implementation projects fail, in large part because just 10 percent of staff are excited about AI adoption. We also shared studies that suggest 29 percent of organizations that operate on a four-day schedule use AI extensively in their operations, compared with just 8 percent of those on a traditional five-day schedule.

If your organization, however, operates in a particularly stressful sector, often suffers from burnout-related employee absenteeism, or has a persistent morale problem that brings down productivity, there are a few data points worth keeping in mind.

For example, in the first North American pilot, researchers found that stress, fatigue, and work-life conflicts had all declined among the participants, while physical health, mental health, sleep hours, work-life balance, and "general life satisfaction" all increased significantly. Employees of participating organizations reported a 69 percent drop in burnout and 32 percent said they were less likely to quit. In the sixty-one-company UK pilot that followed, 71 percent of employees reported lower levels of burnout, and 39 percent reported less work related stress.[2] Companies also saw a 65 percent drop in sick and personal days. According to a 2024 study, the burnout rate among the general employee population is 42 percent but drops to just 9 percent among companies that adopt a shorter workweek.[3]

If you believe your employer, manager, or boss may be persuaded by some of the social benefits of a four-day workweek, share with them how, in the North American pilot, male employees spent 27 percent more time looking after children, and 60 percent of participants said they were better able to combine their jobs with caring responsibilities. Though it's still early, the data suggests that the four-day workweek could be a massive step forward for workplace gender equality by encouraging men to chip in more at home and by leveling the playing field for women at work.

As discussed in chapter 7, the four-day workweek also offers significant environmental benefits, helping organizations achieve their emissions reduction targets. Furthermore, research from the pilot studies and elsewhere shows that when given more time off from work, people are more likely to engage with nature, more likely to reduce their carbon footprint, and more likely to spend time volunteering their time toward causes they care about.

As for the bit about the press, speaking, and publicity opportunities that come from being an early adopter—well, just consider how much you knew about YLaw, SMA, Grand Challenges Canada, Tyler Grange, or any of the other companies featured in this book previously and how much you know of them today. You can also simply run an internet search for news articles about the four-day workweek to see the mountain of media that comes with making the switch (including many authored by Jared).

Finally, as you arm yourself with research that can help persuade your internal decision makers to consider a four-day workweek, keep in mind the number one response we typically received, and be prepared to address it. That response, as mentioned earlier, is something along the lines of "It sounds good in theory, but I have clients/customers/suppliers/other stakeholders that depend on my business five days a week, so it just won't work for us." To combat this common reaction, consider sharing case studies of organizations in the same or similar industries or that are comparable to your company's context or business model.

Throughout this book, we've shared the stories of organizations across a broad spectrum of industries, of varying sizes, and in a range of geographical locations in the hope that you'll find some of those examples comparable to your own organization within these pages. In addition to these case studies, we've compiled examples from across all major industries on our website, www.DoMoreInFour. com/Resources, to help you find situations and organizations that your key internal decision makers may find more relevant. Presenting them with a proven solution to a significant business challenge should at the very least merit some thoughtful consideration and move the conversation from "It wouldn't work for us" to "Maybe it would, under the right circumstances." More on that in step 6.

Step 3: Talk to Your Colleagues

The proverb "If you want to go fast, go alone; if you want to go far, go together," applies to a lot of things in life, and the drive for a four-day workweek—or any employee-driven organizational change, for that matter—is no different.

Though we have spoken with founders who have championed the effort alone and quickly, the overwhelming consensus is that slow and steady wins this race, and collective conversations go a lot further than one person's demands. Building an internal group of advocates can be an effective way of building credibility (ethos) to frame the four-day workweek as a serious operational excellence initiative, not an attempt to take more time off from work. Before you talk to your employer, we suggest talking to your colleagues, sharing some of your thoughts and perspectives on why the four-day workweek could be effective at your organization, and gathering their feedback. Sharing what problems you believe it could solve for your employer in step 1 and sharing some of the research and case studies that demonstrate its effectiveness in solving those challenges in step 2 can help form the basis for these conversations.

Before pitching the idea to the top, you'll want to test the waters and build a consensus lower down the org chart. Start by evaluating colleague interest in not just the concept of a day off but an organization-wide effort to really "do more in four." Contrary to the initial reaction we often receive from employers, when we present this concept to everyday workers, most of them immediately jump to what they might do with the extra personal time without considering the heightened expectations that accompany it. Speaking to your colleagues openly about the kinds of changes that may be required to achieve the same or better outcomes while reducing the workweek is vital to ensuring its success (more on those necessary changes in later chapters).

As you begin engaging in conversation with colleagues, speak with folks from across the organization, not just a handful of close friends on your team. Opening a dialogue with those in different departments, with different degrees of tenure, and with diverse experiences can help you anticipate some of the challenges and opportunities that may otherwise occupy a blind spot. Furthermore, you can tap this informal committee to gain additional perspectives, credibility, networks, knowledge, and enthusiasm as the effort progresses. The more diverse, balanced, and representative of your broader organization this group is, the better positioned you will be to address potential concerns and to present realistic solutions.

Step 4: Come Prepared with Solutions

Now that you've taken time to understand your employer's unique perspective, done research into case studies and best practices, and assembled a four-day week advocacy group in your organization, it's time to start getting serious about the practicalities.

As described earlier, many of today's biggest advocates began as skeptics, so don't be surprised if your initial pitch isn't effective. Perhaps they're worried about how their clients will react (most don't notice), or what the change means for vacation days (many firms keep the same number of weeks but reduce the number of days). Maybe they're concerned with what it means for statutory holidays (most keep a four-day schedule rather than go to three), or what happens if a client calls on the fifth day with an unexpected emergency (see chapter 12 for some creative solutions).

Working with your informal team of internal advocates, you can begin to anticipate some of the likely problems your employer will bring up, and you can brainstorm the solutions you'd offer in response. Work together to think of some high-level or organization-wide challenges your employer might consider barriers to implementation, and ask each participant to come up with other obstacles that are specific to their team or department. Then, work together to stress test various solutions, listing the pros and cons of different approaches. For example, you can compare the benefits and drawbacks of a consistent, organization-wide four-day schedule; a team-specific four-day rotation; and an entirely flexible approach that lets employees design their own workweek.

You may also want to create a *risk register*, which lists all the possible organizational hazards of adopting a four-day workweek that you come up with. That way, you can rank the level of risk by scoring each item according to the severity of its potential impact, its likelihood of materializing, and how reversible it would be if it did. Then, you can start thinking collectively about strategies to mitigate or avoid the most serious ones. For challenges without an entirely clear solution or for those that may take more work to resolve, consider countering the downsides with some data about the potential positive impacts. Seek to demonstrate how a short-term disruption and adjustment period, for example, might be outweighed by the longer-term cost savings on recruitment, retention, and absenteeism. Working with your team, you can also consider when might be an opportune time to present your case for a four-day workweek and when might be the right time to implement it, in light of typical business cycles.

While some elements of the four-day workweek can be standardized, many more are specific to the individual organization, and nobody is better positioned to identify those unique challenges and brainstorm appropriate solutions than people operating within it. By approaching your pitch in this way, you can position yourself to address some of the most immediate, predictable, and common concerns while also demonstrating your seriousness about the matter. Coming prepared with solutions will prove you're already adopting the right mindset and that you're determined to make the change a genuine win–win for the organization and its employees.

Step 5: Frame It as an Incentive, Not a Perk

Much about how the four-day workweek is received is dependent on how it's framed.

On the surface, the four-day workweek sounds like an extremely generous employee perk—and in many ways, it is—but that doesn't tell the whole story. Taking your employer's perspective (pathos), they probably want their staff to be happy, but they probably wouldn't adopt a policy that improves employees' quality of life if it came at the expense of their business's success or viability. In our research—and in our everyday interactions with business owners and employees—we've heard countless stories about how the four-day workweek has improved their lives in dramatic ways. In our experience, however, employers and business leaders are rarely open to adopting such a significant change for those reasons alone. Such benefits tend to factor in later, when an organization considers whether to move from a pilot to a more permanent policy or reviews the change's effectiveness.

While those heartwarming stories about parents who get to be more present in their children's lives or adults who get to spend more time with relatives who live out of state can be incredibly powerful, the time for these stories isn't here and now. For these initial conversations with your internal decision-makers, you'll want to remain focused on organizational outcomes and opportunities. Rather than approaching the four-day workweek as something you're trying to persuade your employer to give you, treat it as an opportunity that you're looking to achieve together to deliver on your organization's loftiest productivity and transformation goals. These aren't extra vacation days written into an employee contract and legally made available; these are weekly performance bonuses, contingent on achieving agreed-upon, measurable targets.

This approach isn't just theoretical or some kind of crafty framing to trick employers, either. Earlier, for example, we explored how SMA had gradually worked its way up from a five-day standard workweek to four and a half days, then to four days, but then reverted to four and a half days again after determining this schedule was a better fit for its current business model. We also briefly described how Adam Husney worked with Joe and his team to implement a four-day workweek at Healthwise to combat a growing attrition rate. Though the policy has remained in place, Adam says it was at one point temporarily revoked. "During one three-month period, we were behind on the delivery of a new product and we suspended the four-day workweek to complete the work," Adam explains, adding that the policy was reinstated once that milestone had been achieved.[4]

When you go to present your four-day proposal, be open and receptive to your boss's need to define clear metrics and redlines to ensure its success and sustainability from a business perspective. Consider asking them directly what kinds of improvements they are struggling to implement and demonstrate how the four-day work-week can give momentum to the changes they're seeking. Be willing to take ownership of the agreed measures of success, accept up front that the program is contingent on hitting these targets or achieving these goals, and be prepared to embrace the collective responsibility and elevated performance accountability that comes with it. How you approach the conversation is likely to determine your effectiveness, and demonstrating a willingness to be flexible will no doubt prove key to securing buy-in.

Step 6: Start Small

Most employers aren't willing to make such a dramatic and permanent change to how they've always done things.

Putting yourself in their shoes once again (logos), consider how steep a hill it is for them to climb from a five-day standard to a workweek that is 20 percent shorter. Rather than asking for that giant leap, break things down into baby steps. In fact, every organization featured in this book started with a smaller change, like a half-day Friday schedule or a four-day workweek pilot in one specific corner of the business, before eventually broadening out to a larger four-day trial or a more permanent policy change. (None, however, have revoked their right to withdraw the policy if certain expectations aren't met.)

If jumping straight into a four-day structure is at the very top of the ladder, the next rung down is an organization-wide pilot framed as a conditional experiment with a fixed time limit. The next level below that is a time-limited pilot on a smaller scale with only specific teams, offices, or departments, rather than an organization-wide change. Fourth from the top is a more incremental pilot that begins with a half-day Friday trial or a nine-day fortnight to gradually ease toward a four-day workweek. One step removed from that is a feasibility study—either conducted internally by HR teams and executives or done by a third party like Joe's firm, Work Time Revolution—to identify the potential opportunities and challenges associated with a four-day workweek without a real-world experiment.

The next option for gradually moving toward a reduced workweek is advocating for changes to business operations in a way that could set the organization up for future adoption, such as advocating for more employee control over work schedules, adopting outcomes-based metrics instead of measuring productivity in term of output over number of hours, implementing focused time blocks, and empowering staff to decline unnecessary meetings (more detail on such strategies in the next chapter). Finally, at the bottom of the ladder is simply inviting a guest speaker, organizing a workshop, or hosting a lunch-and-learn on the subject to offer your leadership and colleagues an expert or pioneering case study. After all, it's a lot harder to say no to a workshop than it is to a 20 percent reduction in working hours.

While the entry point can differ between organizations, many begin with a more formal analysis of the effects of a summer Friday program against certain key metrics, or an extension of that half-day Friday into other parts of the year. During that process, teams can begin to experiment with new strategies for doing more in less time. These steps allow them to chip away at working hours as they simultaneously chip away at organizational waste. If that still feels like a bridge too far for your employer, move to the next suggestion along the spectrum until you find a jumping-off point that feels comfortable for them.

The four-day workweek represents a significant departure from how work has been done for the last hundred years. Even if the arguments outlined in this book resonate with you, it's important to approach the conversation with a certain degree of patience and understanding. After all, it took generations to arrive at the five-day standard, and most attempts to change it haven't yet produced meaningful results. While there are benefits associated with being an early adopter, especially for those who want to use the four-day workweek as a competitive advantage for recruitment and retention, the change probably won't happen overnight.

14 Becoming a Four-Day Organization

Congratulations, you've brought your team on board for a four-day workweek trial! Now what?

As we've stated previously, the productivity gains needed to create the capacity for a four-day workweek won't happen magically or automatically. Making such a drastic change to long-standing workplace practices with little planning or preparation will most likely go over like a lead balloon. That is what we suspect happened to the many organizations that were forced to adopt a remote work policy at the outset of the pandemic and that have since implemented a return-to-office mandate. Of course, the switch wasn't enjoyable. How could it be, when nobody adapted their processes to suit their new reality?

As with remote work, successfully adopting a four-day workweek requires organizations to adopt new tools, technologies, and processes; to help their team members understand and embrace the change; and to empower them to use it as an enabler of higher performance. There are many things that individuals can and should do to make the four-day workweek work for themselves, and we'll explore some of those tactics in the next chapter. Here, we'll outline how organizations can empower their staff to do more in four either by adopting new tools, new processes, and new norms or simply just by getting out of their workers' way. We'll also explore the habits of highly successful four-day organizations, based on Joe's work with hundreds that have made the switch, and share some hard-learned lessons, practical advice, and key steps to help your organization become a four-day one, too.

Are You Ready?

The four-day workweek can't fix a broken culture, at least not on its own.

Instead, we often find that the shorter workweek magnifies an organization's existing cultural strengths and weaknesses. When companies are making the switch, strong workplace cultures tend to get stronger, while weaker ones . . . well, you know. From Joe's intimate work with organizations of various shapes and sizes, he and his team have identified a set of criteria that typically determine whether an organizational culture is well suited to maximize the benefits of a shorter workweek. The first step in making the switch, he suggests, is benchmarking the organization against these cultural traits, operational drivers, leadership mindsets, and approaches to productivity. As you go through the list, consider whether you would rank your organization high, low, or average on each of these criteria.

- *Collaboration:* the level to which the team can effectively collaborate to resolve conflicts and solve problems

- *Intent-based leadership:* the level to which leaders distribute power, ownership, and decision-making with their teams

- *Trust:* the level to which employees are trusted to manage their own work

- *Autonomy:* the level to which there is the ability to self-organize or have control over work patterns

- *Alignment:* the level to which employees' activities are aligned with organizational goals

- *Personal productivity*: the level to which employees manage their own time effectively to achieve goals

- *Accountability:* the extent to which there is collective accountability for performance

- *Outcome focused:* the level to which performance is thought of and measured in terms of outcomes

- *Decision-making:* the extent to which decisions are inclusive, data-driven, and aligned with team goals

- *Innovation:* the level to which teams are encouraged to experiment and test new ideas

- *Growth mindset:* the degree to which individuals are open to new ideas and purposefully seek ways to learn and develop

- *Purpose-led:* the level to which there is a sense of common purpose across the team

If you can check off each of the items listed above as a strong feature of your existing workplace culture, congratulations! You're well positioned to move ahead with a four-day workweek. If some of these concepts feel a bit more foreign to your workplace, or if you think there's some room for improvement, consider spending some time working to address them before moving forward. Not only will doing so better position you for a four-day workweek, but research suggests each criterion is also associated with a more positive and productive workplace environment overall.

The Medium Is the Message

How successful an organization is in its rollout of a four-day workweek program often comes down to how the initiative is packaged, framed, and delivered to participants.

Among the organizations described in previous chapters—including Grand Challenges Canada, SMA, and Geear—some had to reposition the effort to distinguish the fifth day from a typical day off. As many that made the switch ultimately learned the hard way, if it's framed solely as a well-being perk, a vacation day, a recruitment strategy, or similar, the benefits will be fleeting. Eventually, people will settle into their new schedules, expect the extra time off, and feel less obligated to make the necessary—and sometimes difficult—changes that are required to make it successful, not just at the outset but on an ongoing basis. That is why positioning is critical.

The four-day workweek works best when it's framed as an operational excellence project with a built-in incentive that's contingent on achieving predetermined performance objectives. This is not about doing the same work in the same way with increased intensity; it is a fundamental work redesign initiative that requires organizations, teams, and individuals to streamline operations, improve processes, and change work practices. In the pages ahead, we'll explore some of the specific strategies organizations and individuals can implement to truly do more in four.

The question that often remains for leaders is when and how to engage staff in the process. In Joe's experience, there are three key moments that require deeper engagement, on top of the frequent check-ins and assessments that should be part of your typical operations. First is at the *discovery phase*, after leadership has decided to formally explore this initiative. Once that decision has been made, it's best to let your teams know about it early so they can begin to engage with the process. Start with a team briefing or kickoff session to share some of the high-level vision and parameters for the project, and follow with one-on-one interviews, team-wide surveys, and group sessions to dig into the details and unearth some of the key concerns and opportunities.

The next key touchpoint is during the pilot *planning and preparation phase*. After sitting down with individuals and teams to identify key challenges and organizational gaps, you'll want to provide training workshops, expert guidance, and other resources to help address them. This is also where organizations need to clearly communicate how the pilot will work and what they're hoping to accomplish through it. You can also consider establishing cross-functional task groups to help find solutions for specific organizational challenges and concerns that may have been unearthed during the discovery phase.

Finally, it's vital to maintain ongoing communication and coaching during pilot *implementation*. This can include a range of practices, such as anonymous feedback, pulse surveys, one-on-one sessions, small group huddles, daily productivity stand-ups, and an open forum for sharing best practices, successes, and challenges. When you engage your people's assistance in considering what could help them do their work more effectively with such a powerful reward at stake, you unlock all kinds of new ideas and possibilities. The innovation and enthusiasm that this exercise generates is typically worth much more to the organization than what's lost in the time that's given back.

When the four-day workweek is presented as a perk, it will eventually become an expectation. As happened with the five-day workweek, the day may well arrive when the four-day week is the norm for most workers, but that day has not yet arrived. For this reason, today's early adopters need to harness the energy and ingenuity of their people to make it a success. When it's presented as a big challenge with a big reward that needs to be earned every week, everyone becomes collectively motivated to work toward that shared outcome.

It's Not Rocket Science

When Joe challenges teams to identify organizational waste, they often don't have to look very far.

The reality is that much of what we know about wasteful work practices—and more-effective alternatives—is already well established and widely recognizable, despite often feeling out of reach. Tackling meeting bloat sounds obvious, but if it were so easy, everyone would do it. The same goes for eliminating distractions, reducing duplication, automating low-value or repetitive tasks, cutting bureaucratic red tape, and so forth. This is not rocket science; it's simply empowering people to fix what they already know is broken and to streamline what they already recognize is wasteful.

Within most organizations—and especially those with deeply entrenched inefficiencies—however, introducing changes to the way it's always been done can feel herculean. If you have followed the prior steps to ensure organizational readiness and framed the four-day workweek as an operational excellence program with a built-in incentive, your people should be well positioned to start making the productivity-boosting changes they already know could have an impact. Here are some examples of ways leaders can empower their teams to do more in four.

Embrace asynchronous work

For most of human history, collaboration required face-to-face interaction.

Then came early communication technologies like the telephone, and collaboration was suddenly divorced from space, only requiring the parties involved to be available to participate at the same time. Today, we have further evolved to a world in which meaningful collaboration doesn't necessarily need to happen in the same space or at the same time as those we're working with. There will always be a time and place for live, real-time conversations, just as there will always be a time and place in our work lives for direct, face-to-face communication. Nevertheless, we've maintained a long tradition of synchronous communication in a world that no longer requires it for many tasks that we instinctively feel should be handled in real time.

Asynchronous communication has been around for at least as long as the post office, as people could—and frequently did—collaborate across time and space through the mail. Today we've got a lot more tools and technologies that allow us to work together without being in the same place, or on the same schedule, yet there remains a cultural aversion to using them in certain instances. As work becomes more global and more distributed, the ability to effectively collaborate asynchronously becomes more valuable. It would be great if every colleague or client we worked with could be in the same room as us every time we needed them. But being able to effectively work independently—using digital communications for check-ins, questions, and other touchpoints—can enable us to be as effective in less time, as we no longer need to wait for schedules and workflows to align.

Sending an email, a voice note, or even a video presentation may feel less personal, but it is certainly more efficient than pausing a project until you can schedule that real-time interaction. Encouraging teams to embrace more asynchronous work and providing them both the tools and the cultural permission to use them can go a long way in reducing bottlenecks and unnecessary barriers to productivity.

Streamline approvals and decision-making

When there are too many cooks in the kitchen, things tend to get a little spicy.

In most jobs, individuals can only do so much before their progress is impeded by an artificial barrier that requires someone else's attention or approval. While sometimes necessary, these added layers of bureaucracy are just as often built up over time and long outlive their original purpose or necessity. That is especially true in large organizations with lots of hierarchical tiers, but it can also be true in small teams with micromanaging leaders. Not only do all these added tiers impede individual workers' progress, but they also add a load of unnecessary responsibility onto the (often already-overworked) middle managers' shoulders. Streamlining decision-making processes, reducing excessive feedback, and eliminating unnecessary checks and approval layers are effective ways to empower team members and managers to get more done in less time.

To streamline the approval process, leaders should first take a moment to clearly define roles, responsibilities, and decision-making structures for each project or workflow. Then they should encourage their team members to list some of the most common decisions that have to be made to complete their work. Next, have them indicate whether they believe they could make the decision by themselves or think it should be escalated to a manager, indicating whether the decision requires their input, sign-off, or is just for information. That determination should be based on the importance of the decision, the skills and experience of the staff who are deciding, and the potential consequences of getting it wrong. In reviewing the feedback, managers need to put their egos aside and offer an honest assessment of whether their input is additive or creating an unnecessary bottleneck. If the latter, it's time to define the extenuating circumstances or specific conditions that should warrant a check-in in the future, before the manager leaves the rest of the decisions to be made independently.

Note also that this is not a one-and-done exercise, as individual responsibilities, skills, and experience—not to mention the broader business context—are constantly evolving. Ideally, employees should be given more control over their own work and more freedom to progress without oversight as they gain more skills and experience.

This simple exercise has proven broadly effective in cutting unnecessary time spent escalating minor concerns, but it also has the added benefit of creating clarity for frontline staff about what warrants escalation and what doesn't. Without making that distinction, staff will often err on the side of caution and hold up their own work—not to mention their manager's—to seek unnecessary approval before making relatively minor or inconsequential decisions.

Manage your meeting time

And then, of course, there's the world's most obvious time waster: meetings.

Meetings have always been a necessary evil of workplace life, but as the pandemic forced workers into their homes and away from centralized workplaces, organizations overcompensated for the physical distance by going a bit overboard with virtual meetings. According to Microsoft, there has been a 192 percent increase in weekly meetings booked on Teams since 2020.[1] A survey by Asana found that in 2024, executives spent 5.3 hours each week in what they consider unnecessary meetings, up 51 percent since 2019, and managers spend nearly 6 hours weekly in unproductive meetings, up 87 percent since before the pandemic.[2] According to a survey of five thousand knowledge workers across four continents by Atlassian, 72 percent say meetings are ineffective, 78 percent say meeting overload is making it harder to get their work done, and 51 percent report having to work overtime just to make up for time lost to meetings (including 67 percent of those at the director level and above).[3] We all know many meetings could have been an email, so why haven't we figured out a solution?

Canadian e-commerce giant Shopify may have cracked the code. In 2023, the company's executives wanted to encourage a more thoughtful approach to blocking off time in people's calendars. That's what inspired Kaz Nejatian, Shopify's COO and vice president of product, to build the *meeting cost calculator* during one of the company's hack-day events.[4] The tool uses some basic data like the hourly salary of meeting participants, the resources required to host a meeting in person or remotely, and the meeting duration to assign it a dollar figure. For example, Jared's twenty-minute Zoom interview with Kaz and a representative from the company's internal public relations team to chat about this tool came at a cost of $770. According to Kaz, even a half hour meeting with three participants can cost the company $1,600, and removing three meetings per employee each week reduces the total cost of meetings companywide by 15 percent.

Finding ways to simply reduce the time, frequency, and number of participants in meetings can provide significant time savings and, as demonstrated by Shopify, genuine financial savings, too. Consider simply moving your one-hour meetings to 50 minutes, and your

30-minute meetings to 25, to enable better transitions, micro breaks, and mental preparation between each (more on that later). According to Parkinson's law, people will use whatever time you give them, and most will figure out how to cut meeting duration while still accomplishing their intended goal.

While you're at it, ditch the round-robin status updates and move these to an asynchronous alternative like Teams or Slack channels. Make the most out of your meeting time by being clear about what you're gathering for and give staff permission to raise their hand and speak up when they feel they've been invited to a meeting that doesn't benefit from their participation. And if your meeting isn't explicitly designed to solve a problem collectively, to decide something, to learn something, or to bond as a group, just cancel the damn meeting and send an email instead.

Get intentional about communications

One of the first questions Joe asks leaders who are seeking to implement a four day workweek is a simple "What platform does your staff use for communication?" but their answers are often anything but.

In your typical organization—or at least among those that haven't put much thought into it—team members communicate with each other inconsistently, using a broad array of channels and platforms. Your sales team only uses Slack, your legal team only uses email, your engineers are using Teams, and for some reason HR prefers to text. Then there are those that take a kitchen-sink approach, sending a Slack message, waiting five minutes, then following up with a Teams message, then a LinkedIn direct message, then a text message, and finally an email, only to learn that the person they're trying to reach is off that day. Not only is this inconsistent approach to communication exhausting, it's also incredibly distracting, and wasteful.

When Joe and his team audit the collaborative tools and platforms that organizations utilize, he often finds that different teams use different platforms for similar purposes or use the same platforms differently, or both. In smaller organizations, many people engage in what we call *tech dabbling*, using the free trials and limited accounts of a variety of platforms in lieu of a single, unified organizational standard. Virtual meetings, for example, are hosted on Zoom, unless they're likely to go longer than the forty-minute limit imposed on unpaid accounts. Then they're switched to Google Meet, unless they're meeting with a client, in which case they default to Microsoft Teams.

Larger organizations, however, often have the opposite problem; so many of these platforms are optimized for specific functions, and their larger budgets enable them to adopt all at once without defining how and when each should be used. In these situations, individuals have access to paid accounts they rarely use or premium access to platforms they've never even heard of. Not only are these organizations overspending on their communication software, but the lack of uniformity also makes cross-functional collaboration a nightmare.

Having conversations spread across various platforms also makes it nearly impossible to find important information in a timely manner. If you speak to team members on five different platforms, for example, you will probably need to dig through five sources to find that one document you can swear they sent you weeks ago but can't remember if it came via email, Slack, Teams, Asana, Facebook Messenger, WhatsApp, or a LinkedIn message. Having a "single source of truth" for knowledge management not only reduces time wasted sifting through digital files but also helps keep important information organized and accessible.

Using too many platforms can also cause unnecessary distractions. If someone has their Do Not Disturb signal up on Slack or Teams, for example, those using the same platform are a lot more likely to respect their need to focus on work than those who are trying to reach them elsewhere.

So, how do we get everyone on the same page, literally and figuratively? As with approvals and decision-making—and culture, for that matter—the first step is understanding your starting point. Auditing the tech tools used across the organization can help you determine the one platform to rule them all or help you define specific circumstances and cases that would require a specific tool. For example, some groups might want to keep internal communications and project management on Jira, conduct external communications on email, and store key documents and project management on SharePoint. Even if you need to work across multiple platforms, adopting guidelines that set standards around how and when to use each will pay off in the form of fewer distractions, less duplicate work, less time digging for information, fewer artificial barriers between teams and departments, and potentially less money spent on communication platforms that aren't being utilized.

Preparing Your Pilot for Takeoff

When it comes to designing a four-day pilot program, organizations have many key decisions to make, and the most successful organizations include their team members in that process.

Leaders should begin by setting the direction of travel, agreeing on high-level objectives and metrics, and carefully planning messaging and other communication strategies. However, even the most detail-oriented CEO doesn't know the day-to-day intricacies of everyone's jobs well enough to dictate how and where efficiencies can be found. Eventually, they'll need to get their people on board. Depending on the size of your organization, it may be worth starting with a multi-disciplinary task group that is representative of the broader organization. Together you can begin to explore more team-specific targets, opportunities for organizational efficiency, and potential challenges that need to be addressed. This group can also help assess the organization's overall readiness and provide input into key decisions, like the duration and structure of the pilot program.

Once you've set the general guidelines for what you hope to achieve, it's time to get into the nitty-gritty details about how you're going to achieve it. This is where those training exercises mentioned earlier in this chapter come in, focused on areas like workday redesign, effective meeting practices, adopting new productivity tools (or simply streamlining how you use your existing software), empowerment, focus, and prioritization. The specifics of these training exercises will be largely dependent on the organization itself, but this is where individuals and teams ultimately develop effective strategies to do more in four. Organizational leaders should strive to empower individuals to make the necessary changes to their typical work practices to cut waste and to make meaningful, time-saving changes without seeking permission.

Productivity has in some ways become a dirty word in organizations, evoking defensiveness and discomfort. As a result, many teams rarely discuss productivity, if at all, much less engage collectively on how to improve it. One of the most beneficial side effects of pursuing a four-day workweek is opening that dialogue, giving everyone not just permission but also motivation to engage in constructive conversations about quantifying and improving productivity.

Once you've built the runway, it's time for takeoff. As demonstrated in previous chapters, some organizations begin with a more incremental change—such as half-day Fridays or a nine-day fortnight—before eliminating one workday entirely, and that structure has proven successful for many. Throughout the pilot, leaders and managers need to maintain strong lines of communication across the organization. This is where coaching, mentorship, and collaboration are vital. Gathering that feedback early will help leaders troubleshoot, course correct, and pivot if necessary, while making best practices common practice.

15 Your Guide to Doing More in Four

Organizations play an essential role in enabling their teams, but at the end of the day, achieving more in less time requires individuals to play their part.

All the streamlined processes and new workplace standards will have little impact if people aren't developing new habits to accommodate them. As discussed throughout this book, one of the primary advantages of the four-day workweek is that it encourages enthusiastic employee participation in these productivity-boosting initiatives. Without that incentive, unlearning old habits and adopting new ways of working can prove a bridge too far. That is why the shared incentive is so key to the success of the four-day workweek: people really do need to put in the work. If the shortcuts were easy, we'd probably be taking them already.

When it comes to optimizing individual productivity, some of the opportunities for improvement come from the adoption of new tools and technologies, but most require optimizing the equipment that doesn't have a software update: our brains. In the days of the domestic system (or cottage industry), workers would do all the assembly on their own and the results were consequently inconsistent; some workers simply worked faster or created better products than others. During the industrial revolution, production processes were broken down into simple repetitive tasks, with every individual movement on the assembly line carefully studied and optimized for simplicity and consistency.

In our modern knowledge economy, however, we haven't put the same time and energy into optimizing our approach to tasks in a way that best utilizes our natural abilities. Though there is much we still don't know about the human brain, we have learned a lot in recent years about which practices enable our highest levels of cognitive output and which threaten to slow us down. As previously explained by our friend and management professor John Trougakos, things like stress, sleep, nutrition, and breaks have a direct and often-significant impact on our ability to perform at work. And as Leena Yousefi of YLaw also demonstrated earlier in the book, there is only so far the brain can be pushed until it starts fighting back—in her case, in the form of debilitating migraines.

Being more effective at work despite spending less time on the job requires better work behaviors and a concerted effort to optimize our ability to perform. Those seeking to do more in four can aid that effort by unlearning some of their old habits and replacing them with these research-backed strategies and practices.

Audit Your Workday

Most people who have been on a serious diet know that we often don't consider how much we put in our mouths over the course of a day until we're challenged to track it.

When we think about our food consumption on the average day, or even since we woke up this morning, we'll probably add up the calories of our meals and maybe even include a few of the snacks we thought about on our way to the break room. When we're challenged to audit our daily consumption, however, we begin to notice a lot of little items that maybe wouldn't have made the list: the can of soda with dinner, the free samples at the grocery store, the whipped cream topping on our flavored coffee, the bite of dessert that our kids left behind and that would otherwise go to waste. The same is often true of how we spend our time at work. Tracking the big items that make it onto our calendars can help us find efficiencies, but often the biggest gains are found in the little time wasters that fly under the radar.

According to a 2025 survey conducted by Resume Now, 58 percent of workers waste between thirty minutes and one hour of work time per day on distractions like social media, personal emails, and online shopping, while nearly one in five waste at least ninety minutes on nonwork tasks daily.[1] In fact, 53 percent admit to posting selfies or social media updates regularly while at work, and another 41 percent say they do so occasionally.

If you're going to streamline your work, you first need to gain an understanding of how your time is spent, and that includes the stuff that doesn't get blocked off in the digital diary, like conversations and distractions, small personal errands, an extra afternoon coffee break, or a few minutes falling down the social media rabbit hole. We're not saying that these items should be eliminated, but rather that they should be accounted for, to develop an honest assessment of how your time is spent at work. This strategy often reveals some of the wasted calories in our workday—those little snacks of time that feel harmless in the moment but add up over the long run. Much of the transition to a four-day workweek is reliant on maintaining a strict time diet that cuts waste from the calendar, and you can make better use of your own time by homing in on what's taking up the bulk of your day as well as some of those extra minutes around the margins.

Give Every Hour a Mission

Research has found that our physical, mental, and behavioral well-being does not remain consistent throughout the day but rather subscribes to a fairly consistent pattern known as a circadian rhythm.[2]

In his 2018 book *When: The Scientific Secrets of Perfect Timing*, author Daniel Pink outlined how most people experience a mood boost in the morning, a midafternoon trough, and an early-evening recovery.[3] Some, however, also fall into the early-riser "lark" category or the late-night "owl" category, for whom those patterns differ (this book has been written by one of each). For an estimated 80 percent of the population, Pink recommends pursuing analytical tasks in the morning and creative tasks in the late afternoon while saving important decisions for early morning to midmorning to match our energy with the job at hand.

Unfortunately, however, most workers don't get that choice. According to Microsoft's 2025 Work Trend Index, half of all meetings take place between 9 a.m. and 11 a.m. and between 1 p.m. and 3 p.m., precisely when most workers experience those natural productivity peaks.[4]

While these patterns don't hold for everyone, we need to recognize that our moods, motivations, and abilities fluctuate throughout the day and tend to follow typical patterns. You can learn a lot about your own natural rhythms by analyzing your workday map—focusing on your levels of focus, energy, efficiency, and effectiveness for tasks at different periods of the workday—and identifying trends. Many of our most critical tasks are squeezed into whatever slots remain on our calendars after we've allotted time for lower-value activities. Knowing when we're best equipped to accomplish certain tasks allows us to build our focus time around those typical peak performance hours of the day.

When you map out how you'll spend your day at work (a practice that is admittedly time-consuming at first but has a high return on investment), start by writing down when you'll be taking your short and long breaks. Then prioritize and protect blocks to complete your most important work in your highest-energy hours. Once you have breaks and focus time secured, then you can move on to meetings and designated time slots for administrative tasks like responding to email—which Pink would recommend saving for the energy trough, which most experience in the early afternoon. Simply designating that window can also help you maintain focus on the task at hand—such as the analytical work that is recommended for most people in the mornings—knowing there is time to respond to any missed messages later.

Giving every hour a mission allows you to really focus on the tasks that drive results in the hours when you're best equipped to do your best work, without the anxiety of letting other responsibilities slip. This strategy, however, requires allocating time in your calendar for high-priority work and protecting that window as if it were a one-on-one meeting with your CEO. As Joe often says, the only way to protect your time off is to protect your time on. Blocking out hours for heads-down, mission-critical work ensures that you can deliver on what matters most for your organization with energy and vigor while minimizing distractions, all without dropping the ball on lower-priority tasks.

Own Your To-Do List

The word "priorities" is an oxymoron.

The word was adopted into the English language in the 1400s from the Latin, "prioritas," which loosely translates to "first in rank." For the next 500 years the plural form was considered nonsensical, as there could not be more than one first. Its singularity was the point.[5] In just the last century, however, the word "priorities" has been commonly applied to our personal and professional duties, which, by definition, defeats the whole purpose. When we see a daunting task listed alongside a few small easy wins, we tend to prioritize—or rank first—the low-hanging fruit, because who doesn't love crossing stuff off their to-do list?

When that big scary project is just one point below something like reading a report or responding to a few emails, our brains will tell us that these tasks are equal in importance and push us toward the one that feels more achievable. That is why many of the folks who have made the switch to a four-day workweek tell us that it changed their relationship with their to-do list. They say that before making the switch, they felt that everything on the list was of equal importance and needed to get crossed off before they signed off at the end of the day. They also felt that no matter its true importance, every task had to be completed to its highest standard. By assigning urgency to tasks and by giving themselves permission to downgrade low-priority items, many find they're able to better focus on the work that really matters.

When rewriting your to-do list, consider breaking down larger projects into more-reasonable chunks (this approach is often easier in project or task management software than in a written list). All those bite-sized pieces may add a few extra points—or pages—to your task list, but this breakdown will also make each step in a long process feel more achievable. We also suggest assigning a degree of importance to the items on your list, or writing them out in order of importance, to keep the highest-value work top of mind. If you've got a long to-do list, sometimes it's helpful to have a daily plan containing only the three most critical things you want to achieve that day and leave the rest of the list for when those are complete. These strategies ultimately give you subconscious permission to avoid putting gold-standard effort into tasks of bronze-level importance and to reallocate your time and energy to what really matters.

Of course, creating more time to focus on our highest-value work isn't only about reordering an overflowing to-do list. It's also about recognizing that to carve out the space we need for the things that really matter, we also need to engage in *intentional subtraction* and seek organizational permission to deprioritize what is no longer important (or what wasn't actually delivering value in the first place). That's why a four-day workweek typically proves to be a useful excuse to engage in much-needed organizational decluttering.

Increase Focus by Minimizing Disruptions

Have you ever found yourself completely immersed in a task or project, feeling like you're effortlessly firing on all cylinders, as the rest of the world fades away into the background?

It might happen at work once in a blue moon, but many first identify this trancelike state in something they're passionate about and engage in regularly, like painting, playing music, baking a cake, skiing down a mountain, or even playing video games. This feeling is often referred to as a *flow state*, and recent research has found that it enhances performance, improves creativity, and even improves our emotional well-being.[6] The term describes those rare moments when we feel like we're totally immersed in what we're doing, unencumbered by doubt or distraction. In his 2004 TED talk, the late Hungarian psychologist Mihaly Csikszentmihalyi—one of the founders of the positive psychology movement and the person who first identified what he labeled *flow*—described it as the "secret to happiness."[7]

According to Csikszentmihalyi, flow can be best achieved when we're working on something that requires some degree of effort and concentration but isn't overly challenging or demanding; we need to be just the right amount of engaged without tipping toward either boredom or stress. Having a clear goal or objective that we're trying to achieve also helps perpetuate our flow state, and we need to be able to pursue that goal free from distraction. Getting into a flow state is difficult, but getting out of one is as easy as a buzzing phone or the ding of an instant messaging app. That's because even a brief interruption can have lasting effects. According to a study by University of California, Irvine, it takes an average of twenty-three minutes and fifteen seconds for our brains to get back on track after just a mild distraction, in what has become known as the *switch cost effect*.[8] That cost adds up quickly, given that the average worker is interrupted 275 time per day—or every two minutes—by meetings, emails, or pings.[9]

We also often convince ourselves that we're capable of doing more than one thing at once, but research finds the opposite. According to a 2010 study conducted by researchers at the University of Utah's Department of Psychology, just 2.5 percent of the population qualifies as *supertaskers*, or those who can do multiple things at once effectively.[10] For the remaining 97.5 percent of the population, the research suggests that switching tasks too frequently can lead to not just ineffectiveness but also mental and physical fatigue. Rather than trying to do more at once, research suggests we can actually get more done by focusing on one task at a time and avoiding anything that could disrupt our focus. That is why it's so important that, as we strive to make better use of our time, we carve out more opportunities to get into a genuine flow.

The best way to cut down on interruptions is to signal to others that we're not available—and doing so without stopping what we're doing to tell them directly. For those who work remotely, the best way to do that is to simply switch your online status to "busy" on whatever communication platform your team uses the most and abide by the status change yourself. Tempting as it may feel, it's important to avoid clicking on that potentially distracting link or checking your phone during those designated heads-down working windows. In fact, Joe keeps his phone in a lockbox when he needs to shut out distractions and focus. When working in person, having some kind of physical marker on your desk to signal when you're not to be disturbed can also be an effective way to cut down on unnecessary disturbances. Those who work in an open office plan may also want to consider investing in some noise-canceling headphones to help cut down on distracting office sounds.

Make Peace with Imperfection

Ernest Hemingway once struggled to overcome writer's block in the mornings.

We know this because in 1934, an aspiring writer named Arnold Samuelson hitchhiked from Minnesota to Key West to meet his literary hero.[11] Samuelson later wrote that he went all that way hoping for a moment of Hemingway's time; in the end, he wound up living with him for a year as Hemingway's protégé, an experience he would later recount in his 1984 book *With Hemingway: A Year in Key West and Cuba*. During their time together, Samuelson asked Hemingway a seemingly simple question: "How much should you write in a day?" Hemingway, however, found the question so important that he later detailed his answer for *Esquire* magazine in a 1935 interview titled "Monologue to the Maestro."[12] His advice ultimately came down to one key concept. "The best way is always to stop when you are going good and when you know what will happen next," he told the interviewer. "If you do that every day when you are writing a novel, you will never be stuck. That is the most valuable thing I can tell you, so try to remember it."

Hemingway explained that, prior to discovering this technique, he often strived to finish a chapter or a section before ending his day. But he found that the next morning, he struggled to pick up where he had left off. Rather than continuing until he reached a point of exhaustion in pursuit of a sense of completion, only to start what felt like an entirely new task the next morning, he eventually discovered it was more effective to stop midway. "That way your subconscious will work on it all the time," he told *Esquire*. "But if you think about it consciously or worry about it you will kill it and your brain will be tired before you start." This strategy has since become known as the *Hemingway effect*, and it turns out the *Old Man and the Sea* author had tapped into something universal. In fact, recent research proves that the Hemingway effect is real and that we are more motivated to continue working on a task if we feel closer to finishing it.[13] Some of the research into this psychological hack had even begun years before Hemingway met Samuelson.

As Hemingway was struggling to find his groove in the morning as a young writer in Paris, a Lithuanian-Soviet psychologist named Bluma Zeigarnik was unknowingly studying a similar psychological phenomenon.[14] A few years before that, Zeigarnik's professor, psychologist Kurt Lewin, had noticed that waiters had better recall of orders that were unpaid—and that they retained that memory for longer, even after the tab was settled. Orders that were paid for immediately, however, were often quickly forgotten. In 1927, Zeigarnik conducted a series of experiments to determine whether the phenomenon identified by her professor applied outside of the restaurant. In her experiments, Zeigarnik had participants complete tasks in a controlled environment, with some participants stopped halfway through and others allowed to complete the task without pausing. When the participants were asked detailed questions about the tasks hours later, those who had not been able to complete the project had significantly better recall than those who had been allowed to finish.

Just as it's important to carve out dedicated time during our most productive hours to focus on our most important work, it's equally important to allow ourselves the freedom to put our work down before its satisfactory completion. According to what is now described as the *Zeigarnik effect*, not pushing ourselves to the finish line may improve our performance, since our brains naturally dedicate more resources to unfinished business. We're also better at starting something that is partly completed than we are at starting a new task from scratch, as Hemingway discovered soon after this research.

Giving yourself permission to take breaks, to stop working before a task is complete to a high standard, and to start on tasks we know we won't have sufficient time to complete before we need to move on to something else, is key to getting more done in less time. Just because it's 4 p.m. on a Friday (or for those who take Fridays off, Thursday afternoon) doesn't mean it's time to check out. According to Zeigarnik and Hemingway, it may actually be the best time to start something new.

Schedule Strategic Breaks

Like the lithium-ion batteries in our phones and laptops, our brains last longer when recharged more frequently at lower depletion levels.[15]

Studies recommend that to get the most out of your electronic devices' battery pack, recharge them after using 20 to 30 percent of the battery's capacity when possible, and never let it fall below 50 percent.[16] According to John Trougakos, who discussed the science of burnout, motivation, and rest earlier in the book, our brains work much the same way. By not waiting until energy reserves are depleted to rest, his research suggests, employees can reach peak performance levels faster and extend those periods for longer. Of course, much like our electronic devices, we can't always recharge exactly when we need to, but waiting until our own batteries run out will similarly require a longer recharge. A consistent pattern of significant depletion can also reduce our total capacity over time. "When we look at the best types of performance, the evidence is pretty consistent that people generally don't perform at peak levels for super long periods of time," John explains.[17] "They work in clear bursts of productivity, where they're really effective, and then they step away or do things that are less intense to recharge themselves, to then have another go at being really productive." Overall, the data suggests that you can't outsmart your own brain and pushing it to the limit without adequate rest time will result in lower performance. That raises a question: What is the optimal break schedule for enabling performance?

Time Your Breaks

Ensuring that you're taking just the right amount of time off, in the right intervals, can go a long way toward keeping you at your best over the course of a long workday.

According to the latest research, the highest performers often use what's known as the Pomodoro technique.[18] Created in the 1980s by Francesco Cirillo, the technique dictates a precise schedule for break and work time, and the strategy has since been proven effective.[19] The optimal schedule recommended by the Pomodoro technique is approximately 25 minutes of work on a single task, followed by a 5-minute break. After four repetitions of this cycle (or every two hours), the research recommends a longer break of 15 to 30 minutes. Rinse and repeat.

The Pomodoro schedule, however, is just one of several structures that have been found effective. A 2020 study by the makers of a time-tracking and productivity app called DeskTime suggests that the most productive employees work 52 minutes on, 17 minutes off.[20] John's research suggests that most people should seek to achieve peak performance over three 90-minute episodes per day, structured around 50 minutes on, 10 minutes off, 25 minutes on, 5 minutes off, repeated three times a day, with the remaining hours left for lower-value work. Whichever strategy you follow, the key is not to just ballpark it. To adopt this strategy effectively, you need to set some timers and force yourself to stick to the schedule.

The Pomodoro technique doesn't just offer an optimal balance between rest and work, either. In fact, its guiding principle is closely connected to another one we've discussed at length thus far: Parkinson's law. As described earlier, that is the theory that "work expands so as to fill the time available for its completion." The Pomodoro technique leans on this principle by forcing us to break down tasks into 25-minute increments, challenging us to fit as much effort as we can into that limited window. "By segmenting work into distinct Pomodoros," explains Cirillo, "the technique encourages a more conscious approach to time allocation. It allows for more precise tracking of how time is spent on various tasks, fostering better planning and efficiency in both daily tasks and longer-term projects."[21]

The four-day workweek is not intended to be an exercise in work intensification or a challenge to overexert our resources to meet impossible deadlines; that aim would defeat the whole purpose. The four-day workweek is instead a challenge to be more thoughtful about how we spend our time at work, and that goal includes a well-defined, scientifically proven, healthy, and intentional break schedule.

Practice Makes Progress

Grace Tallon, Joe's life and business partner whom we introduced earlier in the book, is a woman of many talents, one of which is the violin.

Grace is the former director of the Newpark Academy of Music in Dublin and continues to play professionally in her new home in Toronto. She says she sees many similarities between her musical training and her practice sessions with small groups in organizations that are making the transition to a shorter workweek. "I can buy the most expensive instrument," she says, "and have the very best teacher money can buy, but if I don't practice every day, I won't be able to play it. The same applies for organizations; you can buy all these wonderful new productivity tools, attend workshops, and work with the best coaches and trainers, but you won't be successful unless you're putting in the work to embed these habits."[22]

Grace explains that breaking old habits is often a lot harder than it sounds. We may find new and better ways of doing things, but if we don't keep doing them, we'll eventually default back to the comfort of our old ways. In fact, research shows that it takes an average of about sixty-six days to replace an old habit with a new one.[23] Learning the violin, like learning how to work more effectively, requires the development of new habits, continuous improvement, and constant reinforcement. "We embed these habits until they're so ingrained that people don't even need to think about them," she says, adding that it's not always an easy task. "It often feels frustrating at the beginning. I'm dealing with very busy people who have done things a certain way for a long time. Most of them just want to go to work, do the best they can, and go home without thinking too much about what they're doing and why."

Changing those habits, Grace says, requires a real commitment on the part of the individual. If they really want that potentially life-changing day off from work each week, however, we know from experience that the vast majority will commit to the process and find ways to improve their personal productivity. To aid in those efforts, she recommends utilizing some new tools that have tapped into human psychology to overcome our old-dog, new-tricks conundrum. Vancouver-based software company Produce8, for example, developed an app inspired by fitness and finance tools to help organizations, teams, and individuals form new workplace habits and build better workdays. The work analytics tool offers insights into the impact of busy work on productivity and well-being, helps users set and achieve workplace goals, and provides daily reports on how work time is spent and where there is room for optimization. In fact, Joe has recently partnered with the company to create a new offering, Focus4, which acts as a personal coach for the workday.

Most people can get from one end of a busy workweek to the other without stopping to think about their productivity. Like the positive impact of collective productivity conversations mentioned before, increasing your individual awareness—and focus on—productivity is an easy step that can produce a significant yield. Simply put, teams that talk proactively about productivity—and individuals who think proactively about their productivity—are likely to be more productive.

As discussed, the most common concern we hear about the four-day workweek is all about meeting client expectations. The second, however, has something to do with the fear that a permanent reduction in work hours will only generate a temporary efficiency boost. If you've been paying attention thus far, however, you know that we strongly encourage organizations to design a four-day program that is structured in a way that encourages continuous improvement.

Individuals, for their part, need to be prepared to put in the work and help find the efficiencies that can make the four-day workweek viable. Adopting the practices outlined here is a great start, but you'll need to remain persistent and keep seeking new ways to boost efficiency. As Grace learned on her way to becoming a professional musician, there is no endpoint for those who truly want to hone their craft. There is no "perfect" that can be achieved and at which point training and learning become redundant. As is the case with playing the violin, practice only makes progress.

16 Our Four-Day Future

When our great-grandchildren look back on this period a hundred years from now, what will they say?

They'll probably suggest it was a time of economic, political, and societal upheaval; a period of rapid change that paved the way for the norms of the next century; and a time of technological advancement, changing economic conditions, and a new relationship with work. If we're lucky, this time will be remembered as the age that undid some of the damage of the industrial era, turning back the clock on the ecological, societal, and workplace sacrifices made necessary by the last period of rapid transition while delivering a more sustainable existence for ourselves, the planet, and our workplaces. One hundred years from now, perhaps people will be telling stories of the first movers, the bold leaders who shunned conventional wisdom and dared to challenge the status quo knowing that history would be on their side.

After a hundred years of industrial-era-like standardization, the pandemic forced us to do things differently. While many have insisted on returning to how things were, that period revealed how there is little holding us to those standards, aside from a lingering belief in their necessity. Now that the illusion has been shattered, we shouldn't just meekly accept the status quo. As we undergo another seismic shift in how work is accomplished—as technology again transforms the way we get things done—history tells us that we have a rare opportunity to set a new standard. Now is the best time to rewrite the rules in a way that better reflects our modern reality, a reality where more-repetitive and more-tedious tasks are handed off to automated tools, putting greater value on our most human traits.

A calculator will keep coming up with the right answer no matter how many hours or days or years it has been operating, assuming the battery is still alive, but our brains are a bit more complex. There is ample research to suggest that, unlike machines, humans can't perform at optimal levels for long stretches of time. Maximizing the performance of the human brain requires rest, balance, and motivation, not more working hours and less autonomy. As AI increases the demand for those quintessentially human traits, both employers and employees will achieve greater outcomes in a world with fewer working hours, not more.

Like the previous wave of lasting changes, efforts to reshape our workplace norms and conventions probably won't come from the political class, at least not until those changes are adopted on a wide-enough scale in the private sector. Remember, the concept of an eight-hour workday was introduced by Robert Owen in 1817 but couldn't overcome the overwhelming opposition at the time. It wasn't until more than a hundred years later, when an opportune moment of upheaval and change presented itself on the other side of the world, that the idea was finally adopted en masse. Now, the eight-hour workday is so ingrained it's hard to imagine any other kind of standard.

Unlike Owen, we are currently experiencing a burst of upheaval and change, of rapid technological innovation and disruption, of changing preferences and perspectives, and a growing demand to reevaluate our relationship with work. If the establishment of the five-day workweek serves as a model, change is most likely to originate in academic papers and picket lines, break room conversations and Slack channels. When it comes to setting a new standard for working hours, history has proven that individual workers and pioneering business leaders have more power to influence lasting change than their politicians.

We believe that the four-day workweek is inevitable—if not in the immediate future, then in the years to come—but the conditions of today happen to be perfectly suited to introduce a departure from long-standing norms. If we don't take advantage now, who knows how long it will be until the next opportunity presents itself.

When Joe began talking about how we had the productive capacity and technological tools at our disposal to move to a four-day workweek, most regarded his belief as a radical concept. More than eight years later, a growing number are finally starting to see it as the most pragmatic response to our current realities.

Despite dramatic increases in productivity over the last century our standard working hours have remained the same, but that doesn't even tell the whole story. Not only are there more individuals per household in the workforce thanks to the rise of female employment, but work itself is no longer contained by practical boundaries. Today, most knowledge workers remain on the job well outside of the standard working hours and their inability to detach from work is having a measurable, negative impact on their emotional wellbeing. In many ways, our workweek hasn't changed in nearly 100 years; in others, it's gotten much longer, as the assembly line workers of the industrial era were never expected to answer a call from work after their shift was done.

The AI era has dawned, and as we enter that brave new world, there will be many competing parties looking to shape our collective futures. There is little doubt our world will change rapidly in the coming years, and we believe the best and most obvious way to align our workplaces with that new reality—to ensure that its benefits are more evenly distributed, and to help solve some of our greatest personal, professional, organizational, and societal challenges—is to reduce the workweek from five days to four. The four-day workweek isn't a cure-all for societal, workplace, and personal challenges, but it does represent an opportunity to make meaningful progress in a way that is additive, not reductive.

If you're an employer struggling to onboard new tools and practices, the four-day workweek can offer your staff a powerful incentive to make radical changes to their work habits. If you're operating in an industry with particularly high burnout rates, highly demanding schedules, or emotionally taxing responsibilities, the four-day workweek offers staff a much-needed respite that will pay itself back many times over in reduced burnout, absenteeism, and turnover. If you're operating in one of an increasing number of highly competitive talent markets or seeking to onboard highly specialized skills, the four-day workweek provides an opportunity to stand out from the crowd, even if you can't afford to outspend the competition. If you operate in a highly creative field, when most of your game-changing ideas arise during off hours, the four-day workweek offers more of that healthy distance from work when the sparks of innovation often ignite. If you're interested in being an employer of choice, enjoying a wave of positive press and boosting employee morale, motivation, and productivity, the four-day workweek offers a proven solution. If you're passionate about building a more balanced world for yourselves and those who come after—to make tangible progress on a range of personal, business, family, community, and societal challenges through a universal benefit rather than a sacrifice—then the four-day workweek is a cause worth championing.

Change is hard, and like any change, this transition won't be easy. However, failing to adapt to changing circumstances and to insist on maintaining an outdated status quo will inevitably prove more challenging than adaptation. We believe that tipping point is imminent.

We have mountains of research that shows that working longer hours doesn't produce better outcomes and can be detrimental in the long run. We have bucketloads of evidence that our culture of equating hours with dedication only inspires performative busyness, not results. We have countless experiments that show how, with the right approach, reducing the workweek can have a positive impact on an organization's overall success across a broad range of metrics. We have a generation of young people who have loudly expressed their need for greater work-life balance. We have access to new technologies that are making us more efficient and effective by the day. All we need is to shed the belief that the workweek must be five days long simply because it was for the last hundred years or so. If we can imagine doing things differently, we can move toward a world of work that offers better outcomes for organizations, individuals, and society at large. So, what are we waiting for?

Notes

Chapter 2

1. Jared Suzman, "The 300,000-Year Case for the 15-Hour Week," *Financial Times*, February 18, 2024, https://www.ft.com/content/8dd71dc3-4566-48e0-a1d9 -3e8bd2b3f60f.

2. Mark Cartwright, "Agriculture in the British Industrial Revolution," *World History Encyclopedia*, March 18, 2024, https://www.worldhistory.org/article/2191 /agriculture-in-the-british-industrial-revolution/.

3. Mark Cartwright and Scott Swigart, "Agriculture in the British Industrial Revolution," *World History Encyclopedia*, March 2024, https://www.worldhistory.org /article/2191/agriculture-in-the-british-industrial-revolution/.

4. Marguerite Ward, "A Brief History of the 8-Hour Workday, Which Changed How Americans Work," CNBC, May 5, 2017, https://www.cnbc.com/2017/05/03/how -the-8-hour-workday-changed-how-americans-work.html.

5. Ward, "Brief History of the 8-Hour Workday."

6. Ward, "Brief History of the 8-Hour Workday."

7. Erin Blakemore, "How America Settled on a 5-Day Workweek," *History*, March 24, 2023, https://www.nationalgeographic.com/history/article/american -workweek-history-explained.

8. Philip Sopher, "Where the Five-Day Workweek Came From," *Atlantic*, April 30, 2018, https://www.theatlantic.com/business/archive/2014/08/where-the -five-day-workweek-came-from/378870/.

9. "Which Countries Have a Friday-Saturday Weekend?," *National*, December 8, 2021, https://www.thenationalnews.com/mena/2021/12/07/when-is-the-weekend-in -the-arab-world/.

10. *New York Herald* editorial, quoted in Erin Blakemore, "How America Settled on a 5-Day Workweek," *National Geographic*, March 24, 2023, https://www .nationalgeographic.com/history/article/american-workweek-history-explained.

11. Henry Ford, "Henry Ford Quotes," *The Henry Ford*, n.d., https://www .thehenryford.org/collections-and-research/digital-resources/popular-topics/henry -ford-quotes.

12. Hasia Diner, "Ford's Anti-Semitism," interview by *American Experience*, *American Experience* (PBS), November 7, 2017, https://www.pbs.org/wgbh /americanexperience/features/henryford-antisemitism/.

13. William M. Blair, "Nixon Foresees 4-Day Work Week; Says G.O.P. Policies Assure Fuller Life for Family," *New York Times*, September 23, 1956, https://www

.nytimes.com/1956/09/23/archives/nixon-foresees-4day-work-week-says-gop-policies
-assure-fuller-life.html.

14. María Luisa Paúl, "Before Sanders, Nixon Pitched Four-Day Workweek," *Washington Post*, March 18, 2024, https://www.washingtonpost.com/history/2024/03/18/four-day-workweek-nixon-bernie-sanders/.

Chapter 3

1. C. Northcote Parkinson, "Parkinson's Law," *Economist*, November 19, 1955, https://www.economist.com/news/1955/11/19/parkinsons-law.

2. Greg Daniels, dir., *The Office*, season 3, episode 3, "The Coup," featuring Steve Carell, Rainn Wilson, Jenna Fischer, John Krasinski, and Melora Hardin, aired October 5, 2006, on NBC Universal Television.

3. Órla Ryan, "'It's Like Having a Bank Holiday Every Week': Trade Union Calls for Four-Day Work Week," *Journal*, September 26, 2019, https://www.thejournal.ie/four-day-work-week-ireland-3-4825941-Sep2019/.

4. Juliet Schor, *The Overworked American: The Unexpected Decline of Leisure* (New York: Basic Books, 1991).

5. Alex Ledsom, "Four-Day Workweek Going Well in U.K., Study Says," *Forbes*, September 26, 2022, https://www.forbes.com/sites/alexledsom/2022/09/26/four-day-work-week-going-well-in-uk-study-says/.

6. Anna Cooban, "Men Did a Lot More Childcare While Trialing a Four-Day Work Week," *CNN*, February 21, 2023, https://edition.cnn.com/2023/02/20/business/4-day-work-week-childcare/index.html.

7. Giulio Piovaccari and Giulia Segreti, "Lamborghini Introduces Four-Day Week for Production Workers," Reuters, December 5, 2023, https://www.reuters.com/business/autos-transportation/lamborghini-introduces-four-day-week-production-workers-2023-12-05/.

8. Sant'Agata Bolognese, "Automobili Lamborghini Signs Draft Agreement for Renewal of Corporate Supplementary Contract," *The NewsMarket*, December 5, 2023, https://www.thenewsmarket.com/news/automobili-lamborghini-signs-draft-agreement-for-renewal-of-corporate-supplementary-contract/s/9d52b105-efd6-41b3-b7cd-fa7d4e60588a.

9. Kari Paul, "Microsoft Japan Tested a Four-Day Work Week and Productivity Jumped by 40%," *Guardian*, November 8, 2019, https://www.theguardian.com/technology/2019/nov/04/microsoft-japan-four-day-work-week-productivity.

10. Thea Watson, "Is the Four-Day Work Week Here to Stay?," *theHRDirector*, May 5, 2024, https://www.thehrdirector.com/business-news/future-of-work/is-the-four-day-work-week-here-to-stay/.

11. Gus Mallett, "Study: Four-Day Workweek Momentum Rises Year on Year," Tech.co, March 19, 2025, https://tech.co/news/four-day-workweek-momentum-rises-yoy.

12. Bernie Sanders, "Thirty-Two Hour Workweek Act," n.d., https://www.sanders.senate.gov/wp-content/uploads/32-Hour-Workweek-Act_Fact-Sheet_FINAL.pdf, endorsed by AFL-CIO, UAW, SEIU, AFA-CWA, UFCW, International Federation of Professional and Technical Engineers (IFPTE), 4 Day Week Global, WorkFour, and National Employment Law Project (NELP).

13. AP News, "Spanish Bill to Cut Workweek to 37.5 Hours Heads to Parliament after Receiving Government Approval | AP News," May 6, 2025, https://apnews.com

/article/spain-workweek-reduction-sanchez-unemployment-2abbbc4354304932d58ef4
16ef1f411e.

14. "Utah Saves Millions on Four-Day Week," *CBC*, October 27, 2009, https://
www.cbc.ca/news/utah-saves-millions-on-four-day-week-1.782455.

Chapter 4

1. Daniel Taub and Hannah Levitt, "Jamie Dimon Sees AI Improving Workers'
Lives Even As It Eliminates Some Jobs," *Bloomberg*, October 2, 2023, https://www
.bloomberg.com/news/articles/2023-10-02/dimon-sees-ai-giving-a-3-1-2-day
-workweek-to-the-next-generation.

2. Matthew Fox, "Billionaire Hedge-Fund Boss Steve Cohen Says a 4-Day
Workweek Is Coming—and It's Part of Why He Made a Big Investment in Golf,"
Business Insider, September 6, 2024, https://www.businessinsider.com/steve-cohen-4
-day-workweek-artificial-intelligence-ai-golf-investment-2024-4.

3. Alexandra Tremayne-Pengelly, "Zoom CEO Eric Yuan Says A.I. Will Make
4-Day Work Weeks a Norm," *Observer*, September 25, 2024, https://observer.com
/2024/09/zoom-eric-yuan-ai-shorter-work-weeks/.

4. Jordan Hart, "Bill Gates Says a 3-Day Work Week Where 'Machines Can Make
All the Food and Stuff' Isn't a Bad Idea," *Yahoo Tech*, November 22, 2023, https://tech
.yahoo.com/business/articles/bill-gates-says-3-day-183643614.html.

5. Bill Gates, video interview with Jared Lindzon, January 6, 2025.

6. Andrew Yang, email to authors, May 2, 2024.

7. Conor Cawley, "The Impact of Technology on the Workplace: 2024 Report,"
Tech.co, January 4, 2024, https://tech.co/news/impact-technology-workplace-report
-2024.

8. "British Workers Could Claw Back 390 Hours of Working Time per Year with
Artificial Intelligence," *Visier*, July 10, 2023, https://www.visier.com/company/news
/british-workers-could-claw-back-390-hours-of-working-time-per-year/.

9. Luiz Garcia, Lukas Kikuchi, and Will Stronge, "GPT-4 (Day Week): US
Edition," Autonomy Institute, November 20, 2023, https://autonomy.work/portfolio
/gpt-4-day-week-us/.

10. John MacFarlane, "AI Could Enable a 4-Day Work Week for a Quarter of
Canadians: Report," *Yahoo Finance*, April 29, 2024, https://ca.finance.yahoo.com/news
/ai-could-enable-a-4-day-work-week-for-a-quarter-of-canadians-report-133141054
.html.

11. James Ryseff, Brandon F. De Bruhl, and Sydne J. Newberry, "The Root Causes
of Failure for Artificial Intelligence Projects and How They Can Succeed: Avoiding the
Anti-Patterns of AI," RAND, August 13, 2024, https://www.rand.org/pubs/research
_reports/RRA2680-1.html.

12. The Adecco Group, *Leading in the Age of AI: Expectations versus Reality*," Adecco
Group, 2025 https://www.adeccogroup.com/business-leaders-research-2025.

13. Abendroth Dias Kulani, et al., "Generative AI Outlook Report," JRC
Publications Repository, June 13, 2025, https://doi.org/10.2760/1109679.

14. "Generative AI Adoption in the Enterprise: The 2025 Writer AI Survey,"
writer.com, 2025, https://go.writer.com/enterprise-ai-adoption-survey.

15. Kim Basile, Michael Bradshaw, and Maryjo Charbonnier, "People Readiness
Report 2025," Kyndryl People Readiness Report, Kyndryl and Edelman DXI, 2025,

https://www.kyndryl.com/content/dam/kyndrylprogram/doc/en/2025/people
-readiness-report.pdf.

16. Leadership IQ, "AI Readiness and the Road Ahead: Understanding Company Preparedness for an AI-Driven Future," Leadership IQ, July 1, 2023, https://www.leadershipiq.com/blogs/leadershipiq/ai-readiness-and-the-road-ahead.

17. Jared Lindzon, "31% of Employees Are Actively 'Sabotaging' AI Efforts. Here's Why," *Fast Company*, March 20, 2025, https://www.fastcompany.com/91302120/employees-are-actively-sabotaging-ai-efforts-heres-why.

18. Lindzon, "31% of Employees Are Actively 'Sabotaging' AI Efforts. Here's Why."

19. John Maynard Keynes, "Economic Possibilities for Our Grandchildren," in *Essays in Persuasion* (New York: Harcourt Brace, 1932), 358–373, https://www.aspeninstitute.org/wp-content/uploads/files/content/upload/Intro_and_Section_I.pdf.

20. Lawrence Mishel, Elise Gould, and Josh Bivens, "Wage Stagnation in Nine Charts," Economic Policy Institute, January 6, 2015, https://www.epi.org/publication/charting-wage-stagnation/.

21. Tom Rees / Bloomberg, "AI Could Enable Humans to Work 4 Days a Week, Says Nobel Prize–Winning Economist," *Time*, April 5, 2023, https://time.com/6268804/artificial-intelligence-pissarides-productivity; Prarthana Prakash, "Nobel Prize–Winning Economist Weighs in on How ChatGPT-Like Tools Are Transforming the Future of Work—1 Year Since Its Launch," *Fortune Europe*, December 2, 2023, https://fortune.com/europe/2023/12/02/nobel-prize-economist-christopher-pissarides-chatgpt-workplace-automation-one-year-launch/.

22. Christopher Pissarides, Google Meet video call with Jared Lindzon on July 15, 2024.

23. Nick Valentine, "The History of the Calculator," *The Calculator Site* (Hazell Industries Ltd.), November 10, 2024, https://www.thecalculatorsite.com/articles/units/history-of-the-calculator.php.

24. Ian Webster, "$1,000 in 1961 to 2025," Inflation Calculator, Official Inflation Data, Alioth Finance, May 15, 2025, https://www.in2013dollars.com/us/inflation/1961?amount=1000.

25. Leslie Wayne, "The Year of the Accountant," *New York Times*, January 3, 1982, https://www.nytimes.com/1982/01/03/business/the-year-of-the-accountant.html.

26. US Bureau of Labor Statistics, "Accountants and Auditors," Employment Data, Occupational Outlook Handbook, US Bureau of Labor Statistics, August 29, 2024, https://www.bls.gov/ooh/business-and-financial/accountants-and-auditors.htm.

27. Kimberly A. Whitler, "New Study on CEOs: Is Marketing, Finance, Operations, or Engineering the Best Path to CEO?," *Forbes*, October 14, 2019, https://www.forbes.com/sites/kimberlywhitler/2019/10/12/new-study-on-ceos-is-marketing-finance-operations-or-engineering-the-best-path-to-the-c-suite/.

Chapter 5

1. Niki Jorgensen, "Performance Punishments: What They Are and How to Avoid Them," *Forbes*, June 16, 2023, https://www.forbes.com/councils/forbeshumanresourcescouncil/2023/06/16/performance-punishments-what-they-are-and-how-to-avoid-them/.

2. Andy Ackerman, dir., *Seinfeld*, season 7, episode 12, "The Caddy," written by Gregg Kavet and Andy Robin, aired January 25, 1996, on NBC.

3. Sue Cantrell et al., "2024 Global Human Capital Trends," *Deloitte Insights*, 2024, https://www2.deloitte.com/us/en/insights/focus/human-capital-trends/2024.html.

4. Atlassian, "The State of Teams 2024," *Work Life* (Atlassian), February 23, 2025, https://www.atlassian.com/blog/state-of-teams-2024.

5. Julian Birkinshaw and Jordan Cohen, "Make Time for the Work That Matters," *Harvard Business Review*, September 1, 2013, https://hbr.org/2013/09/make-time-for-the-work-that-matters; Team at Slack, "New Slack Research Shows Accelerating AI Use and Quantifies the 'Work of Work,'" Slack from Salesforce, February 27, 2024, https://slack.com/blog/news/new-slack-research-shows-accelerating-ai-use-at-work.

6. Asana, "How Work about Work Hurts Productivity," Asana.com, https://asana.com/resources/why-work-about-work-is-bad

7. Cal Newport, "Why Can't We Tame AI?" Cal Newport's Blog, June 6, 2025, https://www.goodreads.com/author/show/147891.Cal_Newport/blog.

8. Microsoft, "Breaking Down the Infinite Workday," June 17, 2025, https://www.microsoft.com/en-us/worklab/work-trend-index/breaking-down-infinite-workday.

9. BambooHR, "The New Surveillance Era: Visibility Beats Productivity for RTO & Remote," BambooHR, June 6, 2024, https://www.bamboohr.com/resources/data-at-work/data-stories/2024-return-to-office.

10. John Trougakos, phone interview with Jared Lindzon, September 19, 2024.

11. Organisation for Economic Co-operation and Development (OECD), "Hours Worked," OECD, n.d., https://www.oecd.org/en/data/indicators/hours-worked.html.

12. John F. Helliwell et al., "Executive Summary," Ch. 1 of *World Happiness Report*, ed. John F. Helliwell et al. (Oxford: Wellbeing Research Centre, 2025), https://worldhappiness.report/ed/2025/executive-summary/.

13. Garrigues, "Reduction of Working Hours: A Global Trend Reaching Latin America," Garrigues, June 21, 2024, https://www.garrigues.com/en_GB/new/reduction-working-hours-global-trend-reaching-latin-america.

14. MND Staff, "Sheinbaum Administration Promises a 40-Hour Workweek by 2030," Mexico News Daily, May 6, 2025, https://mexiconewsdaily.com/news/40-hour-workweek-mexico-2030/.

15. Christopher Pissarides, video interview with Jared Lindzon on July 15, 2024.

16. OECD, "Income Inequality," OECD, n.d., https://www.oecd.org/en/data/indicators/income-inequality.html.

17. Tay Hong Yi, "Shorter Working Hours, Better Upward Income Mobility: 5 Trends among S'pore Resident Workers in 2024," *Straits Times* (Singapore), November 28, 2024, https://www.straitstimes.com/business/economy/shorter-working-hours-better-upward-income-mobility-5-trends-among-spore-resident-workers-in-2024.

18. "Chile: Law Introducing 40 Hours Working Week Entered into Force," *Industrial Relations News*, July 1, 2024, https://industrialrelationsnews.ioe-emp.org/industrial-relations-and-labour-law-july-2024/news/article/chile-law-introducing-40-hours-working-week-entered-into-force.

19. Garrigues, "Reduction of Working Hours."

20. Heather Chen, Yoonjung Seo, and Andrew Raine, "This Country Wanted a 69-Hour Workweek; Millennials and Generation Z Had Other Ideas," *CNN*, March 20, 2023, https://www.cnn.com/2023/03/18/asia/south-korea-longer-work-week-debate-intl-hnk/index.html.

21. Lin Qiqing and Raymond Zhong, "'996' Is China's Version of Hustle Culture; Tech Workers Are Sick of It," *New York Times*, April 29, 2019, https://www.nytimes.com/2019/04/29/technology/china-996-jack-ma.html.

22. Kim Tan, "E-Commerce Company in China Implements 4.5-Day Work Week, Promised No Salary Cuts & Lay-Offs," *MustShareNews (MS News)* (Singapore), January 14, 2025, https://mustsharenews.com/company-china-work-week/.

23. Singapore Ministry of Manpower (MOM), Manpower Research & Statistics Department, "Summary Table: Hours Worked," MOM, released May 21, 2025, https://stats.mom.gov.sg/pages/hours-worked-summary-table.aspx.

24. John P. Trougakos and Ivona Hideg, "Momentary Work Recovery: The Role of Within-Day Work Breaks," in *Current Perspectives on Job-Stress Recovery*, vol. 7, *Research in Occupational Stress and Well Being*, ed. S. Sonnentag, P. L. Perrewé, and D. C. Ganster (Leeds: Emerald Group Publishing, 2009), 37–84, https://doi.org/10.1108/s1479-3555(2009)0000007005.

25. Trougakos and Hideg, "Momentary Work Recovery."

26. Wonpil Jang, et al., "Overwork and Changes in Brain Structure: A Pilot Study," *Occupational and Environmental Medicine*, May 13, 2025, https://oem.bmj.com/content/82/3/105.

27. Jared Lindzon, "Working Long Hours Can Change Our Brain—and Not in a Good Way, Study Shows," the *Globe and Mail*, June 17, 2025, https://www.theglobeandmail.com/business/careers/article-working-long-hours-can-change-our-brain-and-not-in-a-good-way-study/.

28. John P. Trougakos, "A Manager's Guide to Emotional Exhaustion," *Insights Hub* (Rotman), July 2024, https://www-2.rotman.utoronto.ca/insightshub/talent-management-inclusion/managers-emotional-exhaustion.

29. Jeff Wilser, "Why Using All Your PTO Is Good for You (and Your Career)," *Expedia*, June 2024, https://www.expedia.com/magazine/vacation-deprivation/.

30. Shradha Dinesh and Kim Parker, "More Than 4 in 10 U.S. Workers Don't Take All Their Paid Time Off," Pew Research Center, April 14, 2024, https://www.pewresearch.org/short-reads/2023/08/10/more-than-4-in-10-u-s-workers-dont-take-all-their-paid-time-off/.

31. Eva C. Buechel and Elisa Solinas, "The Detachment Paradox: Employers Recognize the Benefits of Detachment for Employee Well-Being and Performance, Yet Penalize It in Employee Evaluations," *Organizational Behavior and Human Decision Processes* 188 (May 1, 2025): 104403, https://doi.org/10.1016/j.obhdp.2025.104403.

32. Marie Martinez et al., "The Health and Economic Burden of Employee Burnout to U.S. Employers," *American Journal of Preventive Medicine*, February 1, 2025, https://doi.org/10.1016/j.amepre.2025.01.011.

33. William J. Fleming, "Employee Well-Being Outcomes from Individual-Level Mental Health Interventions: Cross-Sectional Evidence from the United Kingdom," *Industrial Relations Journal* 55, no. 2 (January 10, 2024): 162–182, https://doi.org/10.1111/irj.12418.

34. John Chan, Sally Clarke, and Amanda Cebrian, "The State of Workplace Burnout 2024," Infinite Potential, 2024, https://infinite-potential.com.au/the-state-of-burnout-2024.

35. PR Newswire, "Corporate Wellness Solutions Market Worth $94.6 Billion by 2026: Exclusive Report by MarketsandMarkets," PR Newswire, June 21, 2021, https://www.prnewswire.com/news-releases/corporate-wellness-solutions-market-worth-94-6-billion-by-2026--exclusive-report-by-marketsandmarkets-301316218.html.

Chapter 6

1. "The 4 Day Week Long-Term Pilot Report," 4 Day Week Global, https://4dayweek.com/long-term-2023-pilot-results.

2. Anisah Hooda-Tarbhai, video interview with Jared Lindzon, July 11, 2024.

3. The Nobel Prize, "The Sveriges Riksbank Prize in Economic Sciences in Memory of Alfred Nobel 2010," n.d., https://www.nobelprize.org/prizes/economic-sciences/2010/summary/.

4. American Psychological Association, "Workers Appreciate and Seek Mental Health Support in the Workplace," American Psychological Association, 2022, https://www.apa.org/pubs/reports/work-well-being/2022-mental-health-support.

5. Frank Weishaupt, "Pulse Survey Data—The New Rules of Work: Why Flexibility, Boundaries, and Technology Define the Hybrid Workplace in 2025," Owl Labs, May 7, 2025, https://owllabs.co.uk/blog/pulse-survey-2025.

6. Hannah Erin Lang, "This Tech Exec Got Backlash for Saying She Was Once 'Willing to Work for Free.' Is It Ever a Good Idea?," *MarketWatch*, July 25, 2024, https://www.marketwatch.com/story/squarespace-exec-got-backlash-for-saying-she-was-willing-to-work-for-free-in-her-early-career-is-it-a-good-idea-for-gen-z-35032dc3.

7. Spriha Srivastava and Sawdah Bhaimiya, "Gen Z Is Prioritizing Living over Working Because They've Seen 'the Legacy of Broken Promises' in Corporate America, a Future-of-Work Expert Says," *Business Insider*, January 19, 2024, https://www.businessinsider.com/gen-z-working-to-live-rather-than-living-to-work-2024-1.

8. Jessica B. Rodell, Braydon C. Shanklin, and Emma L. Frank, "'I'm So Stressed!': The Relational Consequences of Stress Bragging," *Personnel Psychology* 77, no. 4 (March 5, 2024): 1441–1465, https://doi.org/10.1111/peps.12645.

9. Intuit, "Prosperity Index Study," Intuit, January 2023, https://www.intuit.com/blog/wp-content/uploads/2023/01/Intuit-Prosperity-Index-Report_US_Jan-2023-1.pdf.

10. Deloitte, "The Deloitte Global 2024 Gen Z and Millennial Survey," Deloitte, May 14, 2024, https://www.deloitte.com/global/en/about/press-room/deloitte-2024-gen-z-and-millennial-survey.htm.

11. May Goldhacker, "Generation GPT: What Gen Z Really Wants from Work," ATeams, May 6, 2024, https://www.a.team/mission/gen-z-ai-research.

12. Lane Gillespie, "Survey: 89% of American Workforce Prefer 4-Day Workweeks, Remote Work or Hybrid Work," *Bankrate*, August 18, 2023, https://www.bankrate.com/personal-finance/hybrid-remote-and-4-day-workweek-survey/.

13. Hays, "Are We Getting Closer to a Four-Day Working Week?," Hays, London, 2023, https://www.hays.co.uk/documents/d/global/four-day-working-week-report-2023-uk.

14. Randstad, "Work-Life Balance Tops Pay: Randstad's Workmonitor Reveals New Workplace Baseline," Randstad, Diemen, the Netherlands, January 21, 2025, https://www.randstad.com/press/2025/work-life-balance-tops-pay-randstads-workmonitor-reveals/.

15. Raheeb Rahman, video interview with Jared Lindzon, July 8, 2024.

Chapter 7

1. Jon Leland, video interview with Jared Lindzon, April 12, 2024.

2. M. Reuter et al., "Decreasing Emissions of NOx Relative to CO2 in East Asia Inferred from Satellite Observations," *Nature Geoscience* 7, no. 11 (September 28, 2014): 792–795, https://doi.org/10.1038/ngeo2257.

3. US Energy Information Administration (EIA), "Net Generation for All Sectors," Electricity Data Browser, EIA, n.d., https://www.eia.gov/electricity/data/browser/.

4. US Environmental Protection Agency (EPA), "Sources of Greenhouse Gas Emissions," EPA, March 31, 2025, https://www.epa.gov/ghgemissions/sources -greenhouse-gas-emissions.

5. Kyle Knight, Eugene A. Rosa, and Juliet B. Schor, "Reducing Growth to Achieve Environmental Sustainability: The Role of Work Hours," in *Capitalism on Trial*, ed. Jeannette Wicks-Lim and Robert Pollin (Cheltenham, UK: Edward Elgar Publishing, 2013), https://econpapers.repec.org/bookchap/elgeechap/14843_5f12.htm.

6. Jonas Nässén and Jörgen Larsson, "Would Shorter Working Time Reduce Greenhouse Gas Emissions? An Analysis of Time Use and Consumption in Swedish Households," *Environment and Planning C: Government and Policy* 33, no. 4 (January 1, 2015): 726–745, https://doi.org/10.1068/c12239.

7. Douglas Broom, "Four-Day Work Week Trial in Spain Leads to Healthier Workers, Less Pollution," *European Business Review*, October 26, 2023, https://www .europeanbusinessreview.eu/page.asp?pid=6985.

8. Megan Brenan, "Covid-19 and Remote Work: An Update," Gallup, October 16, 2024, https://news.gallup.com/poll/321800/covid-remote-work-update .aspx.

9. Katherine Haan, "Top Remote Work Statistics and Trends," *Forbes Advisor*, June 12, 2023, https://www.forbes.com/advisor/business/remote-work-statistics/.

10. US Census Bureau, "United States Commuting at a Glance: American Community Survey 1-Year Estimates," Census.gov, September 9, 2024, https://www .census.gov/topics/employment/commuting/guidance/acs-1yr.html.

11. Jose Maria Barrero et al., "SWAA February2025 Updates," WFH Research, February 7, 2025, https://wfhresearch.com/wp-content/uploads/2025/02 /WFHResearch_updates_February2025.pdf. This paper is an update of Jose Maria Barrero, Nicholas Bloom, and Steven J. Davis, "Why Working from Home Will Stick," working paper 28731, National Bureau of Economic Research, 2021.

12. "Kickstarter Stats—Kickstarter," June 3, 2025, https://www.kickstarter.com /help/stats.

13. Erica Sweeney, "Study: Brands with a Purpose Grow 2x Faster Than Others," *Marketing Dive*, April 19, 2018, https://www.marketingdive.com/news/study-brands -with-a-purpose-grow-2x-faster-than-others/521693/.

14. George Anders, "Why 8 in 10 U.S. Workers Want Employers' Values to Match Theirs," *Workforce Insights* (LinkedIn), April 19, 2023, https://www.linkedin.com /pulse/why-8-10-us-workers-want-employers-values-match-theirs-george-anders/.

15. B Lab Europe, "What Does the B Corp Certification Mean?," B Lab Europe, February 27, 2025, https://bcorporation.eu/what-is-a-b-corp/what-does-b-corp -certification-mean/.

16. Grace Tallon, phone interview with Jared Lindzon, October 25, 2024.

17. Heejung Chung, *The Flexibility Paradox: Why Flexible Working Leads to (Self-) Exploitation* (Bristol, UK: Policy Press, 2022), https://doi.org/10.51952/9781447354796.

18. Child Care Aware of America, "Child Care at a Standstill: Price and Landscape Analysis (2023)," Child Care Aware of America, May 15, 2024, https://www .childcareaware.org/thechildcarestandstill/#LandscapeAnalysis.

19. Daron Acemoglu, David H. Autor, and David Lyle, "Women and Post-WWII Wages" (summary of "Women, War and Wages: The Effect of Female Labor Supply on the Wage Structure at Mid-Century," working paper 9013, National Bureau of

Economic Research, June 2022), *Digest* (National Bureau of Economic Research), November 1, 2002, https://www.nber.org/digest/nov02/women-and-post-wwii -wages; Linda A. Jacobsen, Mark Mather, and Genevieve Dupuis, "Household Change in the United States," Population Reference Bureau Resource Library, September 25, 2012, https://www.prb.org/resources/household-change-in-the-united-states/.

20. Janell Fetterolf, "In Many Countries, at Least Four-in-Ten in the Labor Force Are Women," Pew Research Center, April 14, 2024, https://www.pewresearch.org /short-reads/2017/03/07/in-many-countries-at-least-four-in-ten-in-the-labor -force-are-women; David Kent, "U.S. Has World's Highest Rate of Children Living in Single-Parent Households," Pew Research Center, April 14, 2024, https://www .pewresearch.org/short-reads/2019/12/12/u-s-children-more-likely-than-children-in -other-countries-to-live-with-just-one-parent/.

21. Carrie Blazina, "For American Couples, Gender Gaps in Sharing Household Responsibilities Persist amid Pandemic," Pew Research Center, April 14, 2024, https:// www.pewresearch.org/short-reads/2021/01/25/for-american-couples-gender-gaps-in -sharing-household-responsibilities-persist-amid-pandemic/.

22. Isabel Jackson, "'On the Cusp of Burnout': Flexible Working Leads Mothers to Take on Greater Share of Childcare Tasks, Study Finds," People Management, May 3, 2025, https://www.peoplemanagement.co.uk/article/1919979/on-cusp-burnout -flexible-working-leads-mothers-greater-share-childcare-tasks-study-finds.

23. Alexandra Olson and Claire Savage, "What's behind the Widening Gender Wage Gap in the US?," AP News, October 16, 2024, https://apnews.com/article /gender-wage-gap-women-pay-latina-work-dce2d7cf2c004dfe5322fffaf5fdbbcf.

24. US Department of Labor, "Full-Time / Part-Time Employment," Women's Bureau, US Department of Labor, n.d., https://www.dol.gov/agencies/wb/data/latest -annual-data/full-and-part-time-employment.

25. Vivian Hunt, Dennis Layton, and Sara Prince, "Why Diversity Matters," McKinsey & Company, January 1, 2015, https://www.mckinsey.com/capabilities /people-and-organizational-performance/our-insights/why-diversity-matters.

26. Sundiatu Dixon-Fyle et al., "Diversity Matters Even More: The Case for Holistic Impact," McKinsey & Company, December 5, 2023, https://www.mckinsey .com/featured-insights/diversity-and-inclusion/diversity-matters-even-more-the-case -for-holistic-impact.

27. Mike Stobbe, "US Births Fell in 2023 to the Lowest Count in More Than 40 Years," AP News, April 25, 2024, https://apnews.com/article/how-many-babies -are-born-us-25d99f438645908e5ed6ae29d3914b89; National Center for Health Statistics (NCHS), "U.S. Fertility Rate Drops to Another Historic Low," NCHS, US Centers for Disease Control, April 25, 2024, https://www.cdc.gov/nchs/pressroom /nchs_press_releases/2024/20240525.htm.

28. Karen Gilchrist, "Falling Fertility Rates Pose Major Challenges for the Global Economy, Report Finds," *CNBC*, March 22, 2024, https://www.cnbc .com/2024/03/22/falling-fertility-rates-pose-major-challenges-for-the-global -economy.html.

29. OECD, "Declining Fertility Rates Put Prosperity of Future Generations at Risk," OECD, June 20, 2024, https://www.oecd.org/en/about/news/press-releases/2024/06 /declining-fertility-rates-put-prosperity-of-future-generations-at-risk.html.

30. Associated Press, "Births in Japan Hit Record Low as Government Warns Crisis at 'Critical State,'" *Guardian*, February 28, 2024, https://www.theguardian.com /world/2024/feb/28/birth-rate-japan-record-low-2023-data-details.

31. Max Kim, "One Nation's Plan for Success: Work Less and Make More Babies," *Los Angeles Times*, September 26, 2024, https://www.latimes.com/world -nation/story/2024-09-26/burnout-and-baby-shortages-behind-south-koreas -growing-4-day-workweek-movement; Max Kim, "South Korea's President Urges Citizens to Have More Babies," *Los Angeles Times*, May 11, 2024, https://www .latimes.com/world-nation/story/2024-05-10/facing-a-national-emergency -a-president-implores-his-citizens-to-make-more-babies.

32. Ahn Sung-mi, "Work-Life Balance or Economic Risk? Korea Debates 4.5-Day Workweek Ahead of Election," *The Korea Herald*, May 13, 2025, https://www .koreaherald.com/article/10486387.

Chapter 8

1. Cameron Heath, video interview with Jared Lindzon, April 30, 2024.

2. Kenneth Rapoza, "One in Five Americans Work from Home, Numbers Seen Rising over 60%," *Forbes*, February 20, 2013, https://www.forbes.com/sites /kenrapoza/2013/02/18/one-in-five-americans-work-from-home-numbers-seen -rising-over-60/.

3. "State of Remote Work 2023," Buffer, n.d., https://buffer.com/state-of-remote -work/2023.

4. Simon Ursell, video interview with Jared Lindzon, April 4, 2024.

Chapter 9

1. Leena Yousefi, video interview with Jared Lindzon, April 8, 2024.

2. Patrick R. Krill et al., "Stressed, Lonely, and Overcommitted: Predictors of Lawyer Suicide Risk," *Healthcare* 11, no. 4 (February 11, 2023): 536, https://doi .org/10.3390/healthcare11040536.

3. Nathalie Cadieux et al., "Targeted Recommendations: Towards a Healthy and Sustainable Practice of Law in Canada," ResearchGate, February 9, 2023, https://www .researchgate.net/publication/368390016_Targeted_Recommendations_Towards_a _Healthy_and_Sustainable_Practice_of_Law_in_Canada.

4. Kate Bravery, Joana Silva, and Jens Peterson, "Global Talent Trends 2024–2025," Mercer, 2025, https://www.mercer.com/insights/people-strategy/future -of-work/global-talent-trends/.

5. British Columbia Ministry of Labour, "Statutory Holidays in British Columbia," January 2, 2025, https://www2.gov.bc.ca/gov/content/employment -business/employment-standards-advice/employment-standards/statutory-holidays.

Chapter 10

1. Polly Campbell, "Get Your Best Ideas in the Afternoon and Take a Short Break to Remember Them," *Psychology Today*, September 14, 2019, https://www .psychologytoday.com/us/blog/imperfect-spirituality/201909/fatigue-you-feel-might -just-boost-your-creativity.

2. Harvard Medical School, "Understanding the Stress Response," *Harvard Health Online* (Harvard Health Publishing), April 3, 2024, https://www.health.harvard.edu /staying-healthy/understanding-the-stress-response.

3. Jeffrey Kluger, "Why You Get Your Best Ideas in the Shower," *Time*, July 18, 2024, https://time.com/6999592/shower-thoughts-best-ideas/.

4. Sara Novak, "Why Do We Get Our Best Ideas in the Shower?," *Discover*, November 8, 2022, https://www.discovermagazine.com/mind/why-do-we-get-our-best-ideas-in-the-shower.

5. Alex Daly and Ally Bruschi, video interview with Jared Lindzon, April 1, 2024.

6. Hailey Murphy, phone interview with Jared Lindzon, May 17, 2024.

7. "How Can the 4 Day Week Benefit Working Parents?," 4 Day Week Global, April 4, 2024, https://www.4dayweek.com/news-posts/working-parents.

8. Alex Daly and Ally Bruschi, "How We Found a Version of a 4-Day Workweek That Fits Our Company," *Fast Company*, January 25, 2024, https://www.fastcompany.com/91015021/how-we-found-version-4-day-workweek-fits-our-company.

Chapter 11

1. Jay Goldman, video interview with Jared Lindzon, October 7, 2024.

2. Tracy Smith, video interview with Jared Lindzon, April 25, 2024.

3. US Bureau of Labor Statistics, "Civilian Unemployment Rate," n.d., https://www.bls.gov/charts/employment-situation/civilian-unemployment-rate.htm.

4. Nathan Reiff, "Historical U.S. Unemployment Rate by Year," *Investopedia*, October 17, 2024, https://www.investopedia.com/historical-us-unemployment-rate-by-year-7495494.

5. Roxanna Edwards and Sean M. Smith, "Job Market Remains Tight in 2019, as the Unemployment Rate Falls to Its Lowest Level since 1969," US Bureau of Labor Statistics, April 28, 2020, https://www.bls.gov/opub/mlr/2020/article/job-market-remains-tight-in-2019-as-the-unemployment-rate-falls-to-its-lowest-level-since-1969.htm.

6. Greg Iacurci, "2022 Was the 'Real Year of the Great Resignation,' Says Economist," *CNBC*, February 1, 2023, https://www.cnbc.com/2023/02/01/why-2022-was-the-real-year-of-the-great-resignation.html.

7. Trading Economics, "United States Job Quits Rate," *Trading Economics*, April 2025, https://tradingeconomics.com/united-states/job-quits-rate.

8. Adam Husney, email interview, responses sent to authors October 16, 2024.

9. "32-Hour Work Week," *Engage* (San Juan County, WA), November 12, 2024, https://engage.sanjuancountywa.gov/san-juan-county-s-32-hour-work-week.

10. US Census Bureau, "2020 Census Will Help Policymakers Prepare for the Incoming Wave of Aging Boomers," Census.gov, October 3, 2024, https://www.census.gov/library/stories/2019/12/by-2030-all-baby-boomers-will-be-age-65-or-older.html.

11. Kris Hudson (media contact), "Demand for Specialized Tech Talent in Artificial Intelligence Surges across North America," CBRE, September 4, 2024, https://www.cbre.com/press-releases/demand-for-specialized-tech-talent-in-artificial-intelligence-surges-across-north-america.

12. Carrie Blazina, "For Today's Young Workers in the U.S., Job Tenure Is Similar to That of Young Workers in the Past," Pew Research Center, April 14, 2024, https://www.pewresearch.org/short-reads/2022/12/02/for-todays-young-workers-in-the-u-s-job-tenure-is-similar-to-that-of-young-workers-in-the-past/.

13. Shalene Gupta, "These Gen Z Employees Have Discovered the Secret to Getting a Bigger Raise—Switch Jobs," *Fast Company*, November 10, 2023, https://

www.fastcompany.com/90979371/gen-z-employees-pay-raises-job-hopping-bigger
-salaries.

14. Shane Wigert and Ben McFeely, "This Fixable Problem Costs U.S. Businesses
$1 Trillion," Gallup, March 25, 2025, https://www.gallup.com/workplace/247391
/fixable-problem-costs-businesses-trillion.aspx.

Chapter 12

1. Chris Leone, video interview with Jared Lindzon, October 15, 2024.
2. Jason Davis and Mark Ophus, video interview with Jared Lindzon, April 1, 2024.

Chapter 13

1. Dawn Klinghoffer and Katie Kirkpatrick-Husk, "More Than 50% of Managers
Feel Burned Out," hbr.org, May 18, 2023, https://hbr.org/2023/05/more-than-50-of
-managers-feel-burned-out.
2. Jan Dönges and Sophie Bushwick, "A Four-Day Workweek Reduces Stress
without Hurting Productivity," *Scientific American*, February 20, 2024, https://www
.scientificamerican.com/article/a-four-day-workweek-reduces-stress-without-hurting
-productivity/.
3. John Chan, Sally Clarke, and Amanda Cebrian, "The State of Workplace
Burnout 2024," Infinite Potential, 2024, https://infinite-potential.com.au/the-state-of
-burnout-2024.
4. Adam Husney, email sent to authors on October 16, 2024.

Chapter 14

1. Microsoft, "Will AI Fix Work?," Work Trend Index Annual Report, Microsoft,
May 9, 2023, https://www.microsoft.com/en-us/worklab/work-trend-index/will-ai
-fix-work.
2. Rebecca Hinds, "The Rise of Unproductive Meetings and the Hangovers They
Leave Behind," Asana, April 8, 2025, https://asana.com/inside-asana/unproductive
-meetings.
3. Atlassian, "Workplace Woes: Meetings Edition," *Work Life* (Atlassian),
January 9, 2025, https://www.atlassian.com/blog/workplace-woes-meetings.
4. David Smith, "Shopify Meeting Cost Calculator," Flowtrace, January 2, 2024,
https://www.flowtrace.co/collaboration-blog/shopify-meeting-cost-calculator.

Chapter 15

1. Keith Spencer, "Time-Wasting Epidemic: 6 in 10 Workers Lose over a Month
of Productivity Every Year to Distractions at Work," Resume Now, March 19, 2025,
https://www.resume-now.com/job-resources/careers/time-wasting-report.
2. National Institute of General Medical Sciences, "Circadian Rhythms," n.d.,
https://www.nigms.nih.gov/education/fact-sheets/Pages/circadian-rhythms.
3. Daniel H. Pink, *When: The Scientific Secrets of Perfect Timing* (Random House:
New York, 2018).
4. Microsoft, "Breaking Down the Infinite Workday," June 17, 2025, https://www
.microsoft.com/en-us/worklab/work-trend-index/breaking-down-infinite-workday.

5. Greg McKeown, "How to Prioritize When Everything Is a Priority," *Entrepreneur*, November 26, 2014, https://www.entrepreneur.com/leadership/how-to-prioritize-when-everything-is-a-priority/240082.

6. David Harris et al., "A Systematic Review and Meta-Analysis of the Relationship between Flow States and Performance," *International Review of Sport and Exercise Psychology* 16, no. 1 (May 27, 2021): 693–721, https://doi.org/10.1080/1750984x.2021.1929402; Nicola S. Schutte and John M. Malouff, "Connections between Curiosity, Flow and Creativity," *Personality and Individual Differences* 152 (August 14, 2019): 109555, https://doi.org/10.1016/j.paid.2019.109555; Remus Ilies et al., "Flow at Work and Basic Psychological Needs: Effects on Well-Being," *Applied Psychology* 66, no. 1 (June 29, 2016): 3–24, https://doi.org/10.1111/apps.12075.

7. Mihaly Csikszentmihalyi, "Flow, the Secret to Happiness," talk at TED2004 Conference, February 2004, YouTube video, https://www.ted.com/talks/mihaly_csikszentmihalyi_flow_the_secret_to_happiness?subtitle=en.

8. Gloria Mark, Daniela Gudith, and Ulrich Klocke, "The Cost of Interrupted Work: More Speed and Stress," in *CHI '08: Proceedings of the SIGCHI Conference on Human Factors in Computing Systems* (New York: Association for Computing Machinery, 2008), 107–110, April 6, 2008, https://ics.uci.edu/~gmark/chi08-mark.pdf.

9. Microsoft, "2025: The Year the Frontier Firm Is Born," Microsoft, https://www.microsoft.com/en-us/worklab/work-trend-index/2025-the-year-the-frontier-firm-is-born.

10. Jason M. Watson and David L. Strayer, "Supertaskers: Profiles in Extraordinary Multitasking Ability," *Psychonomic Bulletin & Review* 17, no. 4 (August 1, 2010): 479–485, https://doi.org/10.3758/pbr.17.4.479.

11. Kevin Dickinson, "Tap into the 'Hemingway Effect' to Finish What You Start," *Big Think*, October 21, 2024, https://bigthink.com/the-learning-curve/the-hemingway-effect/.

12. Ernest Hemingway, "Monologue to the Maestro: A High Seas Letter," *Esquire*, October 1935, https://dianedrake.com/wp-content/uploads/2012/06/Hemingway-Monologue-to-the-Maestro1.pdf.

13. Yoshinori Oyama, Emmanuel Manalo, and Yoshihide Nakatani, "The Hemingway Effect: How Failing to Finish a Task Can Have a Positive Effect on Motivation," *Thinking Skills and Creativity* 30 (February 2, 2018): 7–18, https://doi.org/10.1016/j.tsc.2018.01.001.

14. "Zeigarnik Effect," *Psychology Today*, February 9, 2024, https://www.psychologytoday.com/ca/basics/zeigarnik-effect.

15. Renogy Australia, "Everything You Need to Know about Lithium Battery Charging Cycles," *Renogy* (blog), July 19, 2022, https://au.renogy.com/blog/everything-you-need-to-know-about-lithium-battery-charging-cycles/.

16. F. Hoffart, "Proper Care Extends Li-Ion Battery Life," ResearchGate, April 1, 2008, https://www.researchgate.net/publication/279908080_Proper_care_extends_li-ion_battery_life.

17. John Trougakos, phone interview with Jared Lindzon, September 19, 2024.

18. Francesco Cirillo, "Pomodoro Technique: Time Management Method," Pomodoro Technique, February 8, 2025, https://www.pomodorotechnique.com/.

19. Patricia Albulescu et al., "'Give Me a Break!' A Systematic Review and Meta-Analysis on the Efficacy of Micro-Breaks for Increasing Well-Being and Performance," *PLoS ONE* 17, no. 8 (August 31, 2022): e0272460, https://doi.org/10.1371/journal.pone.0272460.

20. Julia Gifford, "The Rule of 52 and 17: It's Random, but It Ups Your Productivity," Muse, July 31, 2014, https://www.themuse.com/advice/the-rule-of-52 -and-17-its-random-but-it-ups-your-productivity.

21. Cirillo, "Pomodoro Technique."

22. Grace Tallon, phone interview with Jared Lindzon, October 25, 2024.

23. Jeremy Dean, "How Long to Form a Habit? 66 Days Is a Rough Average," *PsyBlog*, November 15, 2024, https://www.spring.org.uk/2024/11/form-habit-66.php.

Index

Acknowledgments

First and foremost, we thank our partners, to whom we owe most of our personal and professional success.

Specifically, Joe thanks his life and business partner, Grace Tallon, without whom this book and the Work Time Revolution would not be possible. Over the past five years, she has charted this voyage together with Joe as a cocaptain—docking in Dublin, anchoring in rural Ireland, navigating New York City, and finally mooring in Toronto. She has made every harbor feel like home through her energy, ambition, and steadfast support.

Jared thanks his wife, Becca, for always encouraging his ambition and professional aspirations, no matter how outlandish, from the moment they met to the moment Joe approached Jared to collaborate on a book, through the production process and beyond. Despite spending most of that time pregnant with their daughter Beatrice, Becca remained a constant source of positive reinforcement, a silent collaborator, and the cheerleader he needed when the going got tough.

Jared also thanks his parents, Susan and Paul Lindzon, who have been a constant source of support through his unconventional career journey. Jared's parents identified the passion he had for writing and journalism at a young age and did everything they could to support and encourage those ambitions as he pursued a freelance career in a notoriously difficult sector.

Outside of our immediate families, we owe the biggest debts of gratitude to our agent, Giles Anderson of the Anderson Agency, and Harvard Business Review senior editor Kevin Evers. Not everyone is willing to stick their necks out for two first-time authors tackling a relatively under-the-radar and—to some—controversial topic. Throughout this process, Kevin and Giles provided valuable feedback, helped us navigate the publishing process for the first time, and advocated for us at every possible turn. Without their efforts, this book would not exist.

Joe also thanks his old boss at Fórsa, Kevin Callinan, who had the foresight and gumption to get behind his vision in this area as early as 2018, when many thought it was a pie-in-the-sky notion, and for supporting his continued journey ever since.

Much gratitude goes to Joe's research collaborator and fellow four-day workweek author Juliet Schor, who in answering the call from a stranger in Ireland to collaborate on studying the impact of the global pilots we've cataloged in this book, catalyzed both a global movement and a lasting friendship.

We also thank the trailblazing leaders and pioneering companies we've documented in these pages and the many others Joe has had the good fortune to work with on shorter-workweek trials and transformation initiatives over the years. We've been inspired by their courageous spirit and have learned a great deal from being so closely exposed to so many truly innovative organizations.

Joe also thanks his partners at Curium Solutions and in particular his friend and colleague Andy Dawson, who were prepared to back such an ambitious and novel idea and have resolutely stayed the course ever since.

Finally, Jared thanks the many editors and publishers who supported his freelance journalism career over the years and helped him gain the experience and confidence necessary to pursue his first book. They include *Globe and Mail* Work Life editor Jordan Chittley, former *Fast Company* deputy editor Kathleen Davis, *Toronto Star* senior business editor Duncan Hood, *Time* senior editor Emma Barker Bonomo, *BetaKit* editor in chief Douglas Soltys, and the many others Jared has had the pleasure of working with over the years at these publications and more.

About the Authors

Joe O'Connor is a globally recognized expert in four-day work-weeks, smart work, and sustainable performance. His mission is to create a future of better work and balanced lives.

He is the CEO and cofounder of Work Time Revolution, a global consulting and research firm that helps organizations redesign work for the age of AI.

His work focuses on building new models of work that reduce overwork, support employee well-being, and drive organizational effectiveness—enabling teams to achieve more while working less.

Joe has designed and led the world's highest-profile, large-scale pilots of the shorter workweek, supporting hundreds of organizations and tens of thousands of employees to increase their productivity and reduce their work time.

He pioneered the first coordinated four-day week pilot in Ireland, codesigned its impact study with researchers from Boston College and University College Dublin, and later scaled the model globally as CEO of 4 Day Week Global, spearheading trials across the United Kingdom, North America, and Australasia.

Originally from County Roscommon in Ireland, Joe now calls Toronto home. He previously served as a visiting research scholar with Cornell University's School of Industrial and Labor Relations (ILR) in New York City, leading a research project on work time reduction. He holds a master's in business strategy and innovation management, a bachelor's in accounting (honors), and an advanced diploma in employment law.

Joe is a frequent media contributor and international speaker on work time innovation, productivity, and workplace well-being. His professional profile can be found on LinkedIn at @joeoconnor990, and at his media portfolio https://linktr.ee/joe.oconnor.

Jared Lindzon is a freelance journalist and public speaker based in Toronto. He is widely recognized as a thought leader on the future of work for his reporting over the last decade. Jared's writing is regularly featured in leading national and global publications, including *Fast Company*, *Time* magazine, the *Globe and Mail*, and the *Toronto Star*, and has been published by the *New York Times*, *Fortune* magazine, and *Rolling Stone*, among others. As a public speaker, Jared often delivers keynote presentations on the future of work and regularly participates in podcasts and panels alongside some of the world's leading business, political, and cultural leaders. Jared earned a master's of arts in journalism and a bachelor's of arts in media studies (honors) from Western University.